BRITAIN IN OLD PHOTOGRAPHS

CHARLTON KINGS

SUSANNE FLETCHER
for the CHARLTON KINGS
LOCAL HISTORY SOCIETY

SUTTON PUBLISHING LIMITED

Sutton Publishing Limited
Phoenix Mill · Thrupp · Stroud
Gloucestershire · GL5 2BU

First published 1999

Copyright © Charlton Kings Local History
Society, 1999

British Library Cataloguing in Publication Data
A catalogue record for this book is available from the
British Library.

ISBN 0-7509-2034-3

Typeset in 10.5/13.5 Photina.
Typesetting and origination by
Sutton Publishing Limited.
Printed in Great Britain by
Ebenezer Baylis, Worcester.

Title page: The date on the drawing from which this is taken is a little obscure, but appears to be 1848. It shows in the foreground an area which is now occupied mainly by the south-eastern part of St Mary's churchyard. New Street did not exist, and the cottages to the left and the centre of the picture are seen as it were from the churchyard path between Horsefair Street and Church Street. They were demolished some time after 1851, when the churchyard was extended and New Street was cut through. The cottages on the right and in the middle distance are in Horsefair Street.

The Charlton Kings Local History Society is a registered charity formed in 1978 to collect and publish historical information about Charlton Kings and to encourage interest in local history generally. In addition to the research undertaken by members, it organises regular evening meetings, outings and social events. Its publications include a History of Charlton Kings, two books of walks round the village, and twice-yearly research bulletins. The subscription is modest, and new members are always welcome. For further information about the society's activities and membership, please contact the chairman, Mrs Mary Southerton, on Cheltenham 520492.

CONTENTS

Charlton Kings in 1924, from a 6 inches to the mile Ordnance Survey map, showing many of the roads and buildings that appear in this book. There have been some obvious changes in the intervening seventy years. The railway line running along the southern perimeter is defunct. The Lilleybrook estate is now a golf course. Most of all, however, there has been a great increase in housing in and around the village. What were then still working farms – Ryeworth, Bafford, Little Herberts, for example – have been built over, as has much of the Charlton Park estate. There are now houses along the east side of Cirencester Road between Cudnall Bridge and the Moorend/Lyefield crossing, and then south of Croft Road. In all this, Charlton Kings is typical of innumerable British towns and villages in that period.

Nearer the centre of the village the 'Fire Engine Station' in Horsefair Street closed many years ago. The 'Diamond Sanitary Laundry' in what was then Moorend Lane has also gone, much more recently. The police station, then in Copt Elm Road, is now in East End Road (and rarely open). The huddle of houses in Church Piece (not named on the map, but between Church Street and Horsefair Street) has been replaced by a car park and shopping precinct.

Finally it is interesting to note that the Ordnance Survey is not infallible. While Holy Apostles' Church is identified by name, the much older St Mary's, in the heart of the village, is (perhaps for lack of space) merely a 'Ch'. And the building marked 'Vicarage' in Horsefair Street had not been an ecclesiastical residence since 1906.

INTRODUCTION

The motorist approaching Cheltenham from London or Cirencester could easily overlook Charlton Kings. There is a rather inconspicuous sign at East End on the London Road; the road from Cirencester has a 'Cheltenham' sign, but none for Charlton Kings. The pattern of housing and shops along the two main roads suggests suburbia rather than a distinct village, and indeed a 1950s Guide to Charlton Kings calls it a 'pleasant residential suburb of Cheltenham'. Away from the main arteries, however, there is a stronger sense of separateness. Round St Mary's Church, in Ryeworth and Ham, in hidden byways, footpaths and culs-de-sac – that is where Charlton Kings is to be found; and even today one can discern the old pattern of small detached settlements, obscured though this is by later development. This ambiguous status, dependent on yet distinct from Cheltenham, epitomises Charlton Kings' history. Certainly the older inhabitants, at least, think of themselves as Charltonians rather than Cheltonians and their pronunciation of the village name – 'Chorlton' – perhaps recalls, even after a thousand years, the original Saxon.

Excavations in 1980 found evidence of Roman and earlier habitation at Vineyards Farm, a mile or so away from the present village. There is no known continuity between that and the Saxon community, the name of which reflects its origin and ownership. A *ceorls tun* was a labourers' settlement. The ceorls provided agricultural labour for Cheltenham Manor, which until 1247 was in royal ownership, hence the suffix 'Kings'. It has been suggested that the earliest Saxon settlement may have been in the Charlton Park area, where the 'big house' of the village was later established. If so, it soon expanded to Bafford, Cudnall, Ryeworth, Battledown and Ham – more names of Saxon origin in use today. Other local names, the 'Ends' (Crab, East etc.), survive from the medieval period of agricultural expansion, each referring to an area of new land being brought into cultivation.

While little of major historical importance seems to have happened at Charlton Kings, the village was not untouched by movement and change, whether on a local or a national scale, and the occasional vivid record suggests that Charltonians were stubbornly independent in their ways and unsympathetic to reforms imposed from outside. There was violent resistance to the enclosure of common land in the sixteenth century. During the next hundred years illegal tobacco-growing flourished here, as in other parts of Gloucestershire, despite the efforts of successive governments to suppress it. The growth of Puritanism seems to have been resisted. One Robert Walker, for a short time minister of St Mary's Church, complained in 1624 of the 'Maypoles on Whitsunday and Church Ales on the Lord's Day with dancing in time of prayer'. This same Walker was dismissed from his cure at Charlton Kings, and appears to have caused an unseemly scene when, resisting his removal, he had to be forcibly restrained from entering the church.

Over the next two hundred years Charlton Kings gained somewhat in gentility, though it retained a rougher element, as will be seen. It benefited from the growing popularity of Cheltenham as a spa, when accommodation for visitors was increasingly in demand. King George III, who came to take the waters in 1788, is said to have visited Charlton Park on several occasions and to have enjoyed 'some good gossip' with Dodington Hunt, the then owner of the property. In due course Charlton Kings, like Cheltenham, became fashionable as a place of retirement for the military, and the solid brick or stucco-faced houses which survive around the village bear witness to the presence of a confident and prosperous Victorian middle class. For the working-class Charltonians, however, life was very different: the years of agricultural depression in the late nineteenth and early twentieth century caused considerable hardship. Some left for the industrial towns, some emigrated, and among those who stayed many families were sustained by the income from the women's work as laundresses, 'taking in Cheltenham's washing'. Those who were better off subscribed to a fund to help special cases of hardship, and the lives of many were made more bearable by the efforts of the more fortunate. Assistance was not only financial, but came through the provision of a good basic education in the Charlton Kings schools and Sunday schools, as well as sports and other activities, often provided under the aegis of St Mary's Church. Reading recollections of village childhood in the years before the First World War, one has the impression of frequent financial poverty, but nevertheless of a richness resulting from growing up in a close community, where one knew and helped one's neighbours.

St Mary's, which became the parish church, originated as a chapel of ease to Cheltenham parish church (also St Mary's), both being subject to Cirencester Abbey. It was consecrated in about 1190, but little of the original Norman building has been left after successive enlargements and alterations. The present tower dates from the fourteenth or fifteenth century, and most of the rest of the visible fabric is Victorian, the result of extensive restoration by the architect John Middleton. Fortunately he was persuaded not to remove the handsome rose window above the west door. The living did not become an independent parish until the early nineteenth century. Since then it has been served by a succession of high-minded and often forceful clergy. None, fortunately, seems to have been in the least like Robert Walker, two hundred years earlier, but the forcefulness displayed by the man who became the first Vicar, James Frederick Secretan Gabb, was exceptional. His obituary in the parish magazine paints a vivid picture both of the man and of the customary amusements of some of the local people in the early 1830s. 'On the Lord's Day, in that part of Charlton Churchyard where his body now lies, the villagers were wont to congregate for badger-baiting, and the village inn hard by had far more attractions for so-called churchmen than the House of God. No one else thought there was much harm in badger-baiting, or that the spot selected for the amusement was too sacred; but this did not prevent the young Curate . . . seizing the badger with his own hands, and amidst the murmurs and threats of his parishioners, putting an end to such desecration of God's Acre.' Unfortunately Gabb blotted his copybook in later years when he had the three-decker pulpit removed from the church: 'the removal of that quaint eighteenth-century erection was . . . the cause of so much heart-burning and abuse that Mr Gabb never ventured on restoration again. It made him cautious and timid to a fault.'

The parish was divided later in the nineteenth century, after Holy Apostles' Church had been built in the angle at the junction of the Oxford and Cirencester roads, not the happiest position in present-day traffic conditions. For its first few years Holy Apostles' was subject to St Mary's, but became a fully independent parish after its belated consecration in 1885. Meanwhile churches of other denominations were appearing. A Primitive Methodist chapel was built in Ryeworth in 1875, and the Baptist church in Church Street a year later. The latter still flourishes, but the Ryeworth congregation is no more, although the building, which was sold in 1956, survives as a private house. Local Roman Catholics did not get their own church until 1957, when Sacred Hearts was built on Charlton Park land.

By the mid-twentieth century Charlton Kings had grown from its small beginnings to a population of over 6,000, well served by schools, numerous shops and public houses, charities, sports clubs and other societies. Though probably most of the working population is employed in Cheltenham or Gloucester, there is some local light industry, mainly on the site of the old railway station off the Cirencester Road and on the industrial estate that replaced the brickworks near Battledown. It might be supposed that the place would be vigorous enough to run its own affairs, but officialdom has decreed otherwise. The excellent Urban District Council, which replaced the Victorian Local Board in the late nineteenth century and carried out its functions efficiently and economically, was abolished in 1974, since when Charlton Kings has been governed by Cheltenham. In the hope of regaining some local autonomy activists demanded and got a parish council in 1995. This, however, has few powers and no jurisdiction over those parts of the village to the west of the Cirencester Road. Charlton Kings' official status as a suburb seems confirmed, yet in spite of all it retains its character. It is hoped that some of its individuality will appear in the following pages.

CHAPTER ONE

ROUND THE VILLAGE

Cudnall Street, c. 1900. The notice on the building on the left advertises the premises of J.W. Cripps, fly proprietor. His advertisement in St Mary's parish magazine around that time states: 'Special attention given to Wedding Orders, at very Moderate Charges. All kinds of Carriages, Broughams, Landaus, Phaetons, at shortest Notice.' It was in one of the houses on the left, just before the entrance to Brookway Road, that Benjamin and Elizabeth James and their family were living in 1851 (see page 111). Higher up Cudnall Street is Hetton Lawn, the house where in 1863 the Revd Charles Lutwidge Dodgson (Lewis Carroll) visited Alice Liddell and her sisters when they were staying there with their grandparents, the Revd and Mrs Henry Liddell. It is said that a mirror over a mantelpiece in the house was the origin of Through the Looking Glass.

The junction of the London and Cirencester Roads, probably before the First World War. The west end of Holy Apostles' Church is in the centre, with the bell-cote of Holy Apostles' School visible in front of it, and, on the pavement just to the right of the tram, the public drinking fountain, all provided through the generosity of Charles Cooke Higgs of Langton House. The tram service came to Charlton Kings in 1903. The rails cannot be clearly seen here, but one of the poles carrying the overhead wires can be seen just behind the tram. The horse-drawn baker's cart on the left is from Margrett and Sons. The houses that now stand on the right on Cirencester Road had yet to be built.

The residents of Haywards Road, which is seen here in 1918, must wish that it were still as free of traffic. The road had been previously known as Field Road and Occupation Road (the reason for the latter name is not known), and it is on the present boundary between Charlton Kings and Cheltenham. The chimney in the distance is that of the Battledown Brickworks, which closed in 1971. The Battledown Industrial Estate now occupies the site.

This postcard of the London Road at Six Ways was posted by D. Hewletts to Miss Hélène Lockhart at a school in Amiens, France, in July 1919. The writer says: 'Do you remember this picture? We think it looks like our trap at Walkers!' Walker's, a baker's and corn chandler's, is the shop in the centre, at the junction with Hamilton Street, with a pillar at the corner – there is a trap parked nearby, but the image is so small that one would have thought accurate identification unlikely. On the extreme left is a post office, with post box set in the wall. Across Overbury Street is the Handy Stores, advertising cocoa (Rowntree's and Fry's), Quaker Oats and Pickwick cigarettes. Next to that is a newsagent's, with a *Daily Mail* placard outside (it is maddeningly impossible to read the news details), and other shops, a bank where Woodliffe's the Chemist's had been briefly a few years before, and, at the end of the row, the London Inn. The gas lamp and the tram lines and overhead wires can clearly be seen. On the other side of the road are the gateposts and walls of some of the large London Road houses. The entrance to Ashley Manor is just out of view. Traffic was not a problem, and a cyclist and horseman could safely stop for a chat in the road.

East End, London Road, just past the junction with East End Road, 1934. On the left-hand side used to be a building used as a mission room during the Revd Thomas Hodson's time as Vicar of St Mary's, but this ceased by 1912 and it became a cottage. It was generally known as the Noah's Ark. After 1929 H. Milward took over both the cottage and the garage next door, and it was used as a small engineering works during the Second World War. Later a petrol company took over and the cottage was demolished. At the time of this photograph the garage also sold teas and ices. Across the road is the Cotswold Inn, which was demolished in the 1960s. Next to it is another garage.

This picturesque view of Greenway Lane in winter is on a postcard which was sent in 1906. The men are
probably clearing the gutters so that melting snow will be able to run away. Greenway Lane still has a fairly rur
aspect, though more houses have been built and it has been suburbanised with two traffic-calming chicanes.

A view of the lower part of Ryeworth Road (the house with the open window on the extreme left is no. 9
probably late 1920s. The view remains much the same today, apart from the addition of traffic, parked cars ar
road markings. Trees and shrubs have grown up more in the front gardens, giving the road a much green
appearance now. The Ryeworth Inn is not visible, but the house just beyond it, which stands a little nearer th
road, can just be seen.

The ford at Spring Bottom, 1890. The River Chelt runs across the road from the right and under the bridge, and the stream in the foreground joins it. The ford, still essentially the same, is usually no more than an inch or two of water across the road for vehicles to splash through. After heavy rain, however, it can swell to a considerable depth, and only recently (in May 1999) a car was washed away under the bridge; the driver was fortunately rescued after a most alarming experience and real danger of drowning. The road across which the river flows is School Road (formerly called Trigmerry Lane and Mill Lane), which runs from Church Street by the Merry Fellow Inn to the London Road.

SPRING BOTTOM, CHARLTON KINGS, CHELTENHAM.
"A winding streamlet, limpid, lingering, slow."
BURROW, CHE

A picture postcard of Spring Bottom, posted in August 1905. It is strange that it does not actually show the ford at all. The children are sitting just about where the water crosses the road. It seems in general to be a somewhat prettified picture rather than an accurate photograph, as the difference between this and the 1890 photograph is so marked. The phrase 'A winding streamlet, limpid, lingering, slow' printed underneath adds to this rather sentimental air, and is certainly not always an accurate description.

This postcard view, dating from the early part of the twentieth century, shows Copt Elm Road, looking from Six Ways towards the centre of the village. The tramlines can be seen on the right curving round from London Road. Copt Elm Road had been cut though in 1865 by the landowner, Sir William Russell, who hoped to sell building plots for substantial houses along its length. The economic situation was not favourable, however, and apart from the 'show houses' he built (Lyefield Villas, at the village end), the only two houses built by 1870 were Lexham Lodge, behind the railings on the left, and Charlton Lawn behind the fence on the right. Lexham Lodge was later used as the Urban District Council offices and is now an NHS mental health resource centre. Charlton Lawn, once the home of the Berkeley family (see page 84) has been divided into flats for many years. The Cotswold escarpment to the south of the village can be seen in the background.

The top of Copt Elm Road from near the war memorial, with the cherry trees in bloom, February 1975. The scene has changed little since then, though the telephone kiosk near the Lyefield Road junction has been replaced by a newer model.

The view from St Mary's Church tower, 1888. On the right is the Royal Hotel, built in 1830. There used to be a garden where its car park is now. The house near the Royal, fronting on to Horsefair Street, was later Sim's bakery, known to children as 'Dicky Doughnut's'. At the time of this picture Croft Road had yet to be built, and Horsefair Street, or the Hollow Way as it was known, can be seen on the left going on up to Timbercombe. In the centre of the picture are lines of washing on the drying grounds, used by the many Charlton Kings women who took in washing from Cheltenham and bigger houses locally. The small building between this and the Royal has gone, and the space is taken by an extension to the pub.

The building of the Working Men's Club is in progress in this picture taken from the top of St Mary's tower. The foundation stone of the club was laid on 18 May 1888 by Captain St Clair Ford. In October 1885 a meeting had been called to establish a Church of England Working Men's Club, and a committee was nominated with Mr Horace Edwards as secretary. A club was established for men of all classes over eighteen years old, to give them 'the means of social intercourse, mutual helpfulness, mental and moral improvement, rational recreation and good fellowship'. It was to be non-sectarian and non-political. At first the club had some rooms in Ruby House, Cudnall Street, but in 1887 the committee was able to buy some land in Church Street for a purpose-built club building. Captain St Clair Ford offered help in designing the building and paying for it. The large upstairs room used for concerts, meetings and other social functions was named the St Clair Ford Hall to acknowledge his generosity. The club was built with bricks from Pilford Brickworks, Leckhampton, and has attractive decorative pargetting round the eaves of the building. The picture also shows a drying ground, on the left, used by laundresses. The school can be seen in the top left corner. The amount of open ground is striking: most of this has now been built over.

Church Street, looking towards the Merry Fellow Inn. On the right is a building which had originally been the first Charlton Kings police station. At the time of the picture, probably the 1930s, it was W. Dale's Stores, also advertised as 'The Noted Bacon Shop'. This block, as far as but not including the bay-windowed shop, which sold ales and stout, was demolished to make way for the precinct. Beyond is the Baptist church, built in 1875.

The top of Church Street on a postcard dated 1962. The houses on the left were demolished in the late 1960s to make way for the precinct. Everything as far as the building which was later Dale's cycle shop was pulled down; there is now a small terrace of modern houses set well back from the street, and then the paved sloping area leading past the library and shops to the Church Piece car park. On the right of the picture can be seen the 1862 almshouses, with Woodbine Cottage on the extreme right. The almshouses, though picturesque, were not very comfortable by modern standards, and in 1970 they were demolished, together with the adjoining cottages, and replaced by Cooper's Court, so called after Samuel Cooper, the original benefactor. Over the roof of the almshouses can just be seen the top of the cupola of the Working Men's Club, which is missing from the picture on page 87.

hurch Street, early 1900s. On the left is Attwood's corn chandler's shop, established, as it says over the door, in 858. Edwin Attwood owned two shops in Church Street; the other is on the extreme left of the photograph, a rocer's and post office. The post box can be seen on the wall, between the windows. Attwood had a coal yard and ables behind the shops, where the garages for Brevel Terrace are now. Edwin Attwood's son, Arthur Lancelot, cceeded him in the business. By 1955 the two shops were still operating, as Morris's general stores and Edgar evely's, grocer's. Now both are gone. There is an insurance office in place of the corn chandler's, and the angtze Chinese take-away in place of the grocer's and post office. Beyond Attwood's hangs the sign of the British orkman. This establishment was set up in 1876 in an attempt to keep working men out of the public houses. It as open in the evenings from 6 to 10 pm. There were armchairs, a table and a fire, while draught boards and minoes were provided, as well as newspapers, though later these were supplied second-hand from the Working en's Club. Smoking was allowed, but no refreshments were available. Not surprisingly this rather cheerless cility could not match up to other attractions, particularly those at the Working Men's Club, and soon after the art of the First World War the British Workman closed. The building was later Wakefield's stores, and is now The ne, an ecumenical café and bookshop. The railings of the Baptist church can just about be seen, then the shop indow of what is now a hairdresser's. The further buildings have gone, making way for modern houses and hurch Piece precinct, before the single-storey shop (formerly Dale's cycle shop) and The Forge newsagent's. On e opposite side of the road, on the extreme right, is a cottage which was demolished in the 1950s, then (with ound glass windows) the 'jug and bottle' department of the Merry Fellow, where beer could be collected for me consumption, then the Merry Fellow itself. This public house had originated in Cudnall Street, and moved to is site in the 1850s. It was said that the beer sold here was 'fighting beer', as distinct from the 'singing beer' ld at the Royal, and the local police were often called in to sort out trouble which had started here. One hastens add that it no longer has this reputation. The lady with the pram is turning into School Road, which was arrower then. The house on the far side of the junction is no longer there.

Charlton Kings used to have a village pump, which was situated on the Forge corner, where the parking space and pillar-box are now. The stocks, which parishes had to provide for the punishment of minor offenders, had at first, from 1763 when they were made, stood outside the south porch of St Mary's Church. They were later moved behind the pump. When the pump was demolished in about 1917–18, the Urban District Council took away the stocks as well and dumped them at the council yard in Horsefair Street. Fortunately Mrs McLaren of Wagers Court took the matter up and made sure they were put back; they were re-erected in their present position (next to the Parish Centre in New Street) and had a shelter put over them. When The Withyholt was demolished in the 1960s, some of its stone tiles were used to renew the roof of the shelter.

art of Horsefair Street, with St Mary's Church in the background, probably late 1890s. The houses on the left, st beyond what is now the car park for Longleat Flats, still remain, looking much the same, except that the one the extreme left is no longer a shop, though its doorway is still across the corner. The house on the far end of e row was later the home of Bert Thornton (1907–92), who was verger of St Mary's Church for the ten years to his death (see page 35). With his faithful dog, he was a familiar figure in and around the church and urchyard. The houses on the right, known as Providence Place, have been demolished, and in their place is the tch of grass alongside Church Piece car park. The local inhabitants look as though life was hard, as indeed it as. It was a time of agricultural depression, and work was short, many families having to rely on what the wives uld earn as laundresses to survive.

posite: This postcard was posted in November 1936. It seems as though it was written by a maid to another in ndon, regretting that 'the Mistress' is unwell and has to stay away longer than planned. She says there is plenty do, with helping her father move plants and washing, but she hopes 'to be straightened by the time you return'. e mentions the 'Weather on Sat[urday]', and that 'the Road is so terrible owing to rain'. The picture shows the ar memorial, commemorating the local people who died in the First World War, and behind it Church Cottage. eyond is Pound Cottage, so called because it stood by the village pound where stray animals were penned. Pound ttage was at one time a public house, and it was said that here one could buy beer by the pound.

The cemetery in Horsefair Street was opened on 20 January 1909 by the Bishop of Gloucester, and this photograph must have been taken not long afterwards. The trees have now grown, giving a much less open appearance than shown here. There was a need for a public cemetery, as the churchyard was almost full, even after its extension in 1884. The parish magazine describes the occasion as 'a ceremony which few of us had ever assisted at before'. A very large crowd had assembled, and with the church bells ringing, 'the choir and clergy, preceded by the two churchwardens with their newly-acquired wands of office, walked in procession to the ground, which they solemnly perambulated, singing Psalms 16, 23 and 130.' The Bishop, standing close to the lychgate, then formally consecrated the ground, the 'sentence of consecration' being read by the registrar (Mr Hannam Clark). This was followed by a short 'but very appropriate' address by the Bishop, the hymn 'On the Resurrection Morning', and the blessing. Afterwards the clergy, choir and members of the District Council were entertained to tea at the Council Hall 'by the kindness of the Chairman of the Council (Mr R.V. Vassar-Smith)'.

Horsefair Street, looking towards St Mary's Church, May 1966. The scene today is little changed, but one would be unlikely to see so few cars parked along the roadside now. The row of cottages on the left remains much the same except for the one with the narrow chimney at the far end of the row, which has been modernised and enlarged. The cottage in the foreground now has a rather fine stone wall instead of the wooden fence shown here. On the right of the picture can be seen the entrance to the cemetery. The houses on the right were built after the demolition of The Grange in 1933, while the houses beyond them, set further forward, have gone and the grass patch by Church Piece car park has taken their place.

Little Herberts Road, New Year's Day 1979. The turning to Beeches Road is on the left. Until the mid-1950s this was part of the farmyard of Little Herberts Farm. The white building in the centre is Southwold Cottage (formerly called Ealing Dene). The houses that can be seen on the left, together with those in Chatcombe Close, were built on the site of Orchard House and its grounds in the mid-1960s. This house was previously called Herbert Villa, and was owned at the end of the nineteenth century by Horace Edwards (1843–1928), who lived there with his wife, son and daughter. He was a printer and stationer, and he also served the local community in many ways. He must have been particularly fond of children, as he provided swings, roundabouts and other attractions in his grounds, and over the years he lived there (he later moved to Battledown) many hundreds of local children enjoyed Sunday School outings there.

The most recent 'real' winter in Charlton Kings was in 1982. This photograph, taken in January, shows part of Ravensgate Road, a scene typical of many side roads at the time. The milkman's van was unable to negotiate the road, and residents left cars at home and walked if they had to go out. Schools were closed for several days and the local children made the most of the opportunities to go sledging on the hills nearby. The houses shown were built by Wimpeys in the mid-1950s and form part of what is known as the Beeches estate. They stand on what was formerly farmland belonging to Little Herberts Farm.

Timbercombe Lane, the continuation of Little Herberts Road and the line of the old Hollow Way, leading to the open country to the south of the village, is here shown in January 1968 under a covering of snow. The photograph shows the lines of elm trees on each side of the lane, which in summer made a tunnel of green.

The same view in December 1976, again under a covering of snow, but after the ravages of Dutch Elm Disease had caused the felling of the trees. The elms have put up fresh shoots again, though these in turn are now showing signs of dying back, and other trees have also grown taller, so the general effect is now much nearer to the 1968 scene once again.

CHAPTER TWO

BUILDINGS

enfall House, near Ham, in a print of 1826. An earlier house on the site was rebuilt in brick between 1799 and 1808, and bought in about 1819 by Edward Iggulden who improved it and landscaped the site. Later owners were Lt. Gen. Molyneux and his family, and Capt. H.G. Willis, after whose death it was bought by Arthur Mitchell, of the brewers Mitchell and Butler. He enlarged the house and introduced Arts and Crafts nelling and furniture. More recently the house was owned by the nuns of the Community of St Peter, and it is now a retreat house belonging to the Diocese of Gloucester.

King's House, photographed here about 1920, probably dates from the seventeenth century. It was called Hawthorne's, after the family which owned it until 1715, but that name was changed to the present one in 1933, though without any historical basis: no monarch has had any connection with the house. It has been remarkably little altered, in spite of having been divided into three dwellings in the early nineteenth century. Fortunately it was bought in the early 1900s by Samuel Holland Healing, an architect, who restored it sensitively to a single house again.

The sitting room at King's House, *c.* 1920, when it was the home of Samuel Holland Healing, of the firm of architects Healing and Overbury.

Wagers Court, *c.* 1906. The house was formerly known as East End Farm, but according to an article in St Mary's parish magazine in 1896 it had been Wagers Court before that. The Wager family lived in Charlton Kings for over 200 years, and one member of the family was Sir Charles Wager (1666–1743), who became First Lord of the Admiralty and subsequently Treasurer of the Navy. Wagers Court was an early sixteenth-century house, but the earliest part, seen here on the right, was rebuilt in 1913–14. The house stands on the corner of Balcarras Road.

Elm Cottage, Brevel Terrace, before the end of the nineteenth century. Beatrice Hopkins is standing outside. She was the wife of Thomas Hopkins, who worked as a gardener. Mr and Mrs Hopkins were the parents of Annie Hopkins (see pages 44 and 117). Elm Cottage still exists, and, unlike quite a lot of local houses, has not had its name changed in the intervening years.

Home Farm, which stood on Little Herberts Road about where the entrance to Morlands Drive is now. It was built by 1500, and used to be called Cherrington's after the family which owned it from the sixteenth century until 1811. It became the Home Farm when Mr and Mrs Lord of Lilleybrook House bought it to add to their estate shortly before 1900. Its purpose then was to provide the Lords' household with milk, eggs and poultry. Eventually the estate was broken up and sold, Lilleybrook House became a hotel, and the farm fell on hard times. It looks such a picturesque rural scene that it makes the decision to demolish the house almost unbelievable, but that is what happened in 1960. It was a great loss.

Bafford Farm, early twentieth century. The building was originally a mill and is referred to as such in the sixteenth century. By the seventeenth century it was a freehold farm. The house remains, but Bafford Approach and the roads leading from it now cover much of the land.

Detmore House, 1880. The house was rented and later bought by John Dobell, a wine merchant, who with his wife Julietta and family went to live there in 1840. The lady in the picture is Julietta Dobell when a widow. The four sons and five daughters were all brought up to be interested in the arts and sciences, and the eldest son, Sydney, was a noted poet, whose work included long epic poems. He was regarded as belonging to the 'Spasmodic School' of poets, so named from their 'over-strained and unnatural sentiment and expression'. Horace, the second son, became a doctor specialising in the treatment of tuberculosis, and two sons, Clarence and Cyrus, continued the wine business, though they were also artistic. One daughter, Alice, married the eminent artist, Briton Rivière RA, at least one of whose pictures can be seen in Cheltenham Art Gallery. Another daughter, Nora, was a skilled photographer, and it is very likely that she took this picture. Detmore House achieved literary significance after Dinah Mulock (the author 'Mrs Craik') visited it. She described the house in her novel *John Halifax, Gentleman*, published in 1857, calling it Longfield.

Another view of Detmore, though the postcard gives it Mrs Craik's fictional name Longfield and prints a quotation from *John Halifax, Gentleman*: 'Our whole hearts were bound up within our own home. . . . Our happy Longfield.' Mrs Craik described Detmore/Longfield as 'the long, low, creeper-covered house', and Eva Dobell (1876–1963), cousin of the poet Sydney Dobell, remarked, in a poem called 'Longfield', how true that was, and mentioned 'Great purple clematis/And white montana scramble to the roof,/And those old-fashioned roses, pink as shells,/Spilling their fragrance from wide-petalled hearts.'

Charlton House, 1906. The picture is taken from a postcard addressed to 'Mrs E. Boyce Podmore, Charlton House', and is from her son, John, who took the photograph. He remarks in his message: 'I think the House makes a very pretty postcard.' The house was rebuilt in about 1810 on the site of a much older one. It was owned by the early nineteenth century by Charles Cooke Higgs, who later had Holy Apostles' Church and School built. The Podmore family lived at Charlton House for some years from 1903 (see page 116). In the First World War the house was used for prisoners of war, and during the Second it became an American Forces HQ. It is now occupied by Spirax-Sarco.

Opposite: The Revd Thomas Hodson, Vicar of St Mary's from 1892 to 1906, his wife and their children in the back garden of The Grange (the Vicarage), *c.* 1900. It stood in Horsefair Street near Church Piece, and the present Grange Field was part of its grounds. It was demolished in 1933. Sitting near the large open window is someone who appears to be a nursemaid, with a baby, most likely the latest addition to the family. Since Charlton Kings began to have resident clergy in the 1830s, they had lived at different addresses, and this was felt to be unsatisfactory. The Revd Charles Dundas had launched an appeal to buy a suitable house, and in 1889 The Grange was purchased for £2,240. It was large, as can be seen, and had a coach house, stables and 3 acres of land.

Box Cottage, Bafford Lane, seen here as it would have looked when it was the home of C. Day Lewis (the future Poet Laureate) from 1933 to 1938. In 1930 Day Lewis had become a master at Cheltenham College Junior School, and two years later had moved with his first wife Mary and infant son Sean to the cottage, for which he had borrowed £600 to buy the freehold. It was while living in Box Cottage, which he described as a 'delectable small house, with its surrounding huge old box hedge', that C. Day Lewis wrote the first of his detective novels, *A Question of Proof*, using the pseudonym Nicholas Blake. This provided money to pay for much-needed roof repairs. C. Day Lewis' decidedly left-wing views, and some of his published poems, offended the College authorities, making his teaching post untenable. He resigned in 1935 to devote his time to writing and to political activities. He actively campaigned for the unsuccessful Labour candidate in Cheltenham, Elizabeth Pakenham (now Lady Longford) in the 1937 General Election, but by the following year he had decided to give up active politics, and he and his family (by now with a second son) moved to Dorset in August 1938 (see also page 107).

Moorend Park, shown here on a postcard posted in October 1902, was built in 1835–40 by Frind Cregoe Colmo
At his request, J.B. Papworth's original design was amended to give it a Swiss-looking exterior. The photogra
shows the ornate conservatory, which does not appear in later photographs. The Colmore family owned
considerable amount of property in Birmingham from 1536 onwards. After the death of Charles Colmore in 178
all of whose children were childless, the estate was divided between his surviving daughter Caroline and a friend
his, Francis Charles, third Marquess of Hertford. Caroline Colmore lived in Cheltenham, where she died in 183
and was buried in the churchyard of St Mary's, Charlton Kings. She settled her estate on her friend Frind Creg
who belonged to a Cornish family, on the understanding that he would adopt the name Colmore. Frind Creg
Colmore had little chance to enjoy life in his Swiss-style house, as he died in 1839. His heir was Colmore Fri
Cregoe Colmore, who married twice and had four children. His heir William Barwick Cregoe Colmore died
1918, and much of the remaining estate in Birmingham (some had already been disposed of) had to be sold to p
death duties. Meanwhile Moorend Park passed out of the family, becoming a military hospital in the First Wo
War and a hotel in the 1920s.

By the time this photograph of the front of Moorend Park was taken the building had become a hotel. A hotel brochure, undated but probably published in the late 1920s or early 1930s. describes it as 'after the picturesque style of an Italian Chalet' (rather than Swiss), and mentions its lovely grounds, with a lake, vineries and a large kitchen garden among other features. Inside, mention is made of 'Electric light, hot and cold running water laid on to all bedrooms, nine up-to-date bathrooms, general central heating supplemented by gas-fires in the bedrooms, lock-up garages and excellent stabling'. The hotel closed in the 1970s, and, most unfortunately, was demolished. The Pinetrees and Shrublands development was built on the site, and Charlton Kings lost one of its most distinctive buildings.

This photograph of the dining room of the Moorend Park Hotel gives an indication of the quality of the interior of the building. The same brochure as mentioned in the caption above states that Moorend Park is 'celebrated for its cuisine. The high degree of excellence attained is due directly to the fact that only the very best of everything English, prepared by a first-class French chef, is served at table.' Examples of the prices are: 'Board Residence and Ordinary Attendance from 4½ guineas a week, or 15s a day', 'Table d'hôte Dinner 5s', 'Afternoon Tea 1s 3d'.

The garden side of Lilleybrook House before 1922, when it became a hotel (first the Lilleybrook Hotel, now the Cheltenham Park Hotel). The house previously on the site was destroyed, apart from the stable block, by a fire in 1831 and rebuilt in 1848. It was bought by John Thornely, who came from Yorkshire, and after his death and his wife's it was inherited by the three daughters of his cousin, the eldest of whom, Mary Ollivant Dugdale, bought out her sisters' shares. She married Herbert Owen Lord, and the house was held in trust for her. Mr Lord was Master of the Cotswold Hunt. Class distinction was still very marked, and an old man remembered that his sisters and all the village girls were instructed at school that whenever they saw Mrs Lord in the village, walking to church, they must curtsey to her. The Lords were generous in support of local charities, and they opened their grounds for the annual Flower Show until the First World War (see page 78). The estate was broken up in 1921–22, the Lords moved away and the house became a hotel. It was commandeered for use by American military forces in the Second World War.

Before the Second World War there were plans for a bypass for Cheltenham. The proposal was to take a route from the A40 between Whithorne and Coxhorne Farm, up Balcarras, past Sappercombe Cottage, and thence to Bradley Road and across Cirencester Road. Lilleybrook Golf Club objected, however, and before the matter could go further the war intervened. Bradley Road was the only stretch which was built. It was named after the builders, Bradleys of Swindon. They had bought Fuller and Maylam's Nursery and built, in addition to Bradley Road, Okus Road and these houses on Cirencester Road. The houses are built from concrete blocks which were made at the firm's Swindon works. The blocks for the interior walls were made on site from compressed sand and other constituents, which were dried under tarpaulin.

CHAPTER THREE

CHURCHES

St Mary's Church in a print from The Gentleman's Magazine, *1823. The church's history dates back to
1190. The tower probably dates from c. 1390–1400, and has been a landmark at the centre of the village
since then. The church as shown here was shortly to acquire its north aisle and rose window.
Later in the nineteenth century further restoration, extensions and alterations produced the building more
or less as we see it today.*

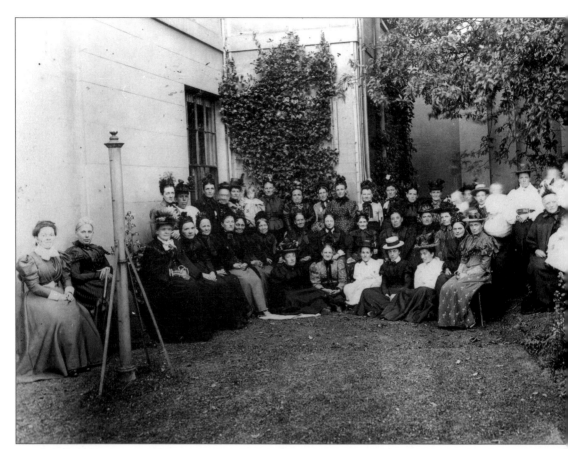

In July 1898 members of St Mary's Mothers' Meeting were entertained to tea at Bafford House by Mrs Bagn
They had, according to a report in the parish magazine, 'a most enjoyable time'. These gatherings were an ann
event, but the 1898 occasion was rather special for being recorded in this photograph. As the parish maga?
remarked: 'Not the least among the pleasures of the afternoon was that of being photographed in a most effec
group by Mr Bagnall whose artistic skill in this art is well known.' The Mothers' Meeting convened each Mon
at 2 pm at the Vicarage. It was distinct from the Mothers' Union, a local branch of which had been founded in
parish in 1892 and which met quarterly. Mr and Mrs W.H. Bagnall, who lived at Bafford House, were very ac
in their support of St Mary's Church and many charitable causes. In 1916 they gave £100 to St Mary's to m
their golden wedding, and in 1922 electric light was installed in the church in memory of Mr Bagnall by
widow and family. Mr Bagnall served as churchwarden for nine years. He was always ready to give lantern s
shows to local organisations, views of Tewkesbury or Gloucester, for example, or seaside scenes. We do not kn
which lady in the photograph is Mrs Bagnall, but she could well be the one on the extreme left. Of all the la
she looks the most 'at home'. The purpose of the curious pole in the foreground is a mystery.

The Revd Thomas Hodson, Vicar of St Mary's from 1892 to 1906, was a hard-working, serious-minded and most conscientious man. He cared deeply about his parishioners, worrying about their immortal souls and the ways they spent their time. He was instrumental in promoting all kinds of purposeful, healthy and educational activities and in setting up such groups as the Church Lads' Brigade, the Men's Help Society, art classes and the Choral and Orchestral Society, as well as encouraging regular church attendance and Christian family life. His wife Catherine was active in running the Mothers' Union branch, and, among other things, organising rummage sales and acting as a District Visitor. She was also involved with entertainments, performing dramatic readings and recitations. She wrote the words of a song, 'Faithful Tommy', at the time of the South African War. The music for this was written by W.H. Brasher, the organist at St Mary's, and the song was performed at a Choral Society concert. Copies were sold to raise money for the organ fund, though not many can have been sold as the amount raised was only 12s 6d! A poem about 'Charlton Church Bells', which appeared in the parish magazine signed C.A.H., is likely to be her work as well. In the large Hodson family sons predominated, three of them later following their father into the Church. The Hodsons lived at The Grange (see page 27), and parishioners were invited to walk in the grounds during summer evenings (except during times of church services). Though Hodson was a serious man, he said 'I dislike gloom, but let us have rightful joy; and religion alone . . . can bring in a reasonable order of things . . . for bringing cheerfulness with the daily life.'

St Mary's Church, with funeral drapes in place to mark the death of King Edward VII in 1910. It was the custom to use such drapes for funerals at this time. When the Revd J.F.S. Gabb was Vicar (1834–75) he had a confrontation with a parish clerk who had been appropriating the drapes after funerals and selling them. Gas had been used for lighting the church since 1862, and the photograph shows the gas standard lamps in the chancel. These were replaced later, in 1914–15, by pendant gas lights, and in 1922 by electric lighting.

The interior of St Mary's Church, 1920 On the right of the chancel arch is the war memorial tablet, inscribed with the names of those from the parish who fell in the First World War. At the top of the arch is the rood, which was designed by George Ryland (see pages 56 and 77), also as a war memorial. The old gas standards had by this time been replaced by inverted incandescent pendant gas lights. Two years later electric lighting was installed. The hymn numbers, from the Ancient and Modern edition used then, are for 'O Trinity, Most Blessed Light', 'Holy, Holy, Holy, Lord God Almighty', and 'Thy Hand, O God, has Guided'. The first is an evening hymn, the numbers would relate to the previous Sunday evening's service – quite likely one of the many Sundays after Trinity.

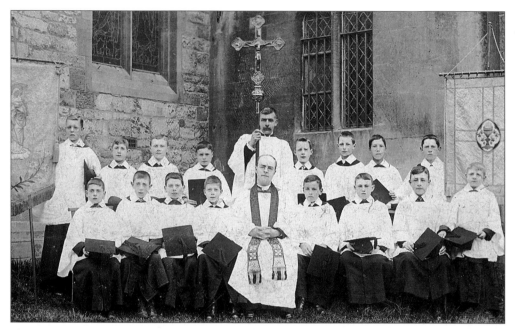

This picture was taken in 1906 on a date between Tuesday 27 November, when the Revd Edgar Neale succeeded Thomas Hodson as Vicar, and Christmas Day. We know this because it was on Christmas Day 1906 that the choirboys exchanged the mortar boards seen here for 'collegiate caps'. The caps had the letters CKC on the front and were worn with pride by the choristers – see, for instance, the picture on the next page. Edgar Neale sits in the centre, with Walter 'Carlo' Fry holding the cross behind him.

St Mary's Church choir, 1978. Back row, left to right: Paul Munday, David Williams, Rob Collier, Ken Collier, Nigel Hill, David Phillips, Les Paine, Alan Wheeler, John Hall, James Campbell, Mervyn Roberts, Harry Stoneham. Fourth row: Brian Clarke (Churchwarden), Bert Thornton (Verger), Peter Burton, Mark Kingston, Colin Kingston (Sacristan), Tim Ramsey, William Nutland, George Rutland, Eric Coleridge (Churchwarden). Third row: Keith Nutland, Frank Wood, Ron Palin, John Mills, the Revd Roland Rempey (Hon. Curate), the Revd Noel Baker (Curate), the Revd David Yerburgh (Vicar), the Revd Keith Jones (Curate), Malcolm Brinson (Organist and Choirmaster), John Blackwell, Mike Nevin, Richard Kicks. Second row: Timothy Griffin, Philip Keegan, William Fletcher, David Atkinson, Michael Wilson, David Mogg, Simon Fletcher, Paul Thornton. Front row: Adam Baker, David Richards, Andrew Burton, Duncan Richards, Raymond Blackwell, Roger Minett, Michael Hill, Guy Kingston, Paul Hill.

The choir and servers of St Mary's Church about to set off for an outing to Malvern, 31 July 1913. They hav
assembled for the photograph before making an early start, as can be seen from the church clock. The Vicar, th
Revd Edgar Neale, with boater and buttonhole, is in the centre of the group and a curate, the Revd Seymou
Chance, next to him wearing a shovel hat, is looking rather doubtful about the whole enterprise. The senio
curate, the Revd Edward Gardner, was to join the party later for lunch 'at George's'. The parish magazine repor
that 'a triumph of persuasion had induced him to spend an hour (but no more) with festive choirboys'. From th
apprehension on Mr Chance's face, this was probably a good move. He, poor man, left the parish on healt
grounds in February 1914, having stayed only a year, and moved to take what was described as 'some very ligh
work in Leigh-on-Sea, Essex'. To the right of the Vicar is a friend of his, Mr Hunt, also wearing his boater. Th
uniformed charabanc driver, Mr Smith, has been included in the photograph. Just over a year after th
photograph was taken the First World War began, and a good number of the young men in the photograp
enlisted, some not to return. Near where the group is standing there would later be the parish war memorial, an
also the lych-gate, which was erected as a thank-offering for peace at the end of that conflict. The boys in th
photograph include Fred Cox, Fred Mason, Harry and Wilfred Sly, Ralph Brocklebank, Cyril Bailey (son of J.
Bailey of Copt Elm Road, a well-known local photographer), Bert Hicks, Bert Mason and Ron Taylor.

is group of smartly dressed young men is St Mary's Young Men's Bible Class, *c.* 1913. The group was at that
ne led by Mrs F.J. Fry, wife of the Headmaster of the Boys' School, and meetings were on Sunday afternoons at
15 in the Parish Room. Back row, left to right (only surnames known in many cases): Harding, A. Bloxham, -?-,
Neather, Hubert Butler, Strickland, Bent. Middle row: Phipps, F. Dyer, -?-, Harper, Roberts, Wilson, Attwood,
Bush. Front row: Larner, Hopkins, H. Dyer, F. Phipps, Williams, Horace Cleevely, Smith, Drake. By 1915 a
umber of these young men had enlisted to fight in the First World War. For example, Horace Cleevely had joined
tchener's Army. He was later taken prisoner, but returned safely and became verger of St Mary's Church for
any years. He died in 1977 aged eighty-six. His son, Alan, has just completed five years as Churchwarden.
ubert Butler's story was a sadder one. He joined the Army very young and lost his life in September 1915, aged
ly just seventeen. The Revd Edgar Neale paid particular tribute to him in a sermon at St Mary's which was
ported in the parish magazine: 'His friends tried to dissuade him from enlisting at such an early age, but he went
cause he said he simply could not stand idly by while others were doing their duty for King and Country.' Neale
ent on to say that Hubert had been a 'choirboy, member of the Boys' Guild and server at our altar', and saluted
s 'stainless life' and 'glorious death': 'It is good for us to have had him with us for these few short years.'

A Charlton Kings Scouts' summer camp, early 1920s. The local troop had been formed in 1910, and it was t
custom to have a camp each year at Pershore, Bredon or some other venue a similar distance away. The sen
scouts would go the day before to pitch camp, taking all the tents and supplies on a large handcart. Bicycles wou
be piled on the top and the scouts would push the cart, taking turns to ride the bicycles. A party of parishione
from St Mary's would have a trip out one day to visit the scout camp, led by the Vicar, and including families
scouts or well-wishers, or those simply wanting a day out. The scout on the right of the picture is wearing t
traditional scout uniform, including the characteristic 'Mounties' hat', which is no longer required headge
There are plenty of splendid hats being worn by the visitors. Back row, left to right: (Charabanc driver), -?-, -
Fred Mason, Edgar Clevely, rest unidentified. Middle row: E.J. Fear, -?-, -?-, Mrs Cooper, Mrs Fear, the re
unidentified. Front row: Mrs Homer and her daughter, Mrs Williams, -?- -?-, the Revd Edgar Neale (and his do
the Revd Leonard Smith (Curate), Mrs Protherough (of Brevel Cottage) and her daughter Phyllis, Dorothy Willia
(later Mrs Bannister), Mrs Neather and her daughter Hazel (later Mrs Parkes), -?-. It is very likely that one of t
older ladies pictured is Mrs Mary Anne Griffiths of Oakfield, Battledown, as she is known to have usually join
these trips. She was the widow of William M. Griffiths, who died in 1902. She was involved in many social a
charitable events, and took a great interest in the local scout troop, giving them financial support when necessa
During the First World War some members went to her house for French lessons. She let them camp in tents
her lawns, and was known to them as the 'Fairy Godmother'.

In June 1893 a dedication service at St Mary's Church (followed by a 'substantial tea') marked the adding of two new bells and the recasting of two others. To mark the occasion a band of the Cheltenham and District Guild of Ringers 'succeeded in ringing a true and complete set of grandsire triples containing 5,040 changes in 3 hours and 18 minutes'. The peal was conducted by Mr William Dyer, who appears in the picture shown here, taken twenty-six years later, and showing those who took part in the Victory Peal in 1919 to celebrate the ending of the First World War. Back row, left to right: H. Halford, T. Dyer, M. Hicks, G. Walters, W. Yeend. Front row: R. Hemming, W. Dyer (Umpire), the Revd E. Neale, J. Ballinger (Conductor), G.F. Pearce.

A group of St Mary's bellringers ringing handbells outside the Working Men's Club, Christmas 1948. Third from the left is R. Hemming, who is also in the 1919 Victory Peal picture, taken almost thirty years before. George Simmons, second from the left, went on to become tower captain and was still ringing some thirty years after this photograph was taken. Although bellringers have always given their services, at one time, the 1913 St Mary's Yearbook (and other years before and after that date) states, 'A subscription list is sent round the parish at Christmas'. This has not happened for many years, but there is still an enthusiastic band of bellringers, and handbells are still rung for such events as the Christmas Fair at St Mary's.

The St Mary's 'Parochial Excursion', as it was described in the parish magazine, photographed by a Persho
photographer on 21 July 1909. This was the second such outing, the first having taken place the previous ye.
The excursion left Charlton Kings at 12 noon in brakes for Tewkesbury. Mr Bathurst's 'magnificent new steam
King' had been chartered. It left Mythe Docks at 2.30 pm and took the party up the Avon to Pershore. The
followed a 'sumptuous tea in picnic style on the meadow by Pershore weir', after which there was time to wand
round the 'quiet old town'. Some went to Evensong at the Abbey. Then they returned to Tewkesbury and depart
for home from the Bell Hotel. The party reached Charlton Kings just after midnight, having had a 'very delight
day's outing'. In the photograph the Vicar, the Revd Edgar Neale, in his boater, stands in front of the funnel of t
steamer.

Opposite: A photograph taken outside St Mary's Hall, after its official opening by Lady Dixon-Hartland, 20 Ap
1927. The Vestry Hall, built in the late 1850s opposite St Mary's Church in New Street, was in a very poor sta
A parish hall was badly needed, and in June 1926 St Mary's acquired the Vestry Hall, then owned by the Board
Guardians. Lady Dixon-Hartland of Ashley Manor gave the £275 purchase money and another £265 towards t
cost of enlarging and refurbishing the building, the total cost being £1,098. Back row, left to right: Mr Freega
(Churchwarden), Mr Gurney Catherine, Mr Peacey, G. Hamlett, F.J. Fry, J. Villar (Architect), Mr McLare
Mr Billings (Builder). Front row: Miss Bullock, Mrs Freegard, General R.G. Burton, Lady Dixon-Hartland, the Re
Edgar Neale, Miss Smith, Miss Fry. The hall was further improved and extended in 1984, being re-opened
St Mary's Parish Centre in March 1985 by the Revd Robert Deakin, Bishop of Tewkesbury and former Vicar
St Mary's.

The Revd Edgar Neale, Vicar of St Mary's, with his choirboys' football team, *c.* 1912. He was extremely proud of his choir, which did indeed have a high reputation, and trained it himself. He was himself a good musician, and he gave great encouragement to the choirboys, with practices each evening and services taking up most of Sunday. There were also annual treats, outings and prizegivings to look forward to, and the football team to belong to or support. The Vicar took a great interest in the boys' well-being. His patience was often sorely tried, and one ex-choirboy remembers him becoming 'quite aereated with us boys' sometimes. However, when boys found themselves in trouble with the local constabulary, and there was a fine to pay, he would invariably plead for them and pay the fine if necessary, recovering it from the errant boy's choir pay.

The Revd Edgar Neale as a young man, photographed in Tewkesbury, presumably while he was curate there, before coming to Charlton Kings as Vicar in 1906. He remained until 1937, and his thirty-one years' incumbency is still remembered by some as a 'golden age'. He was a bachelor, lived simply and devoted all his time to the Church. He acted as choirmaster and played the organ, and he greatly enjoyed the choir's outings and Christmas parties; in fact enthusiasm and enjoyment seem to be words often used about him. During the First World War he wrote and sent parcels to those former choirboys and Bible Class members in the armed forces, and was visibly saddened by the losses. He inherited a High Church tradition and continued it, though with discretion. He was in general a 'larger than life' character, with a voice that could be heard from one end of the village to the other as he cycled round the parish, and seems to have been universally popular.

The Revd Thomas Carlyle Joseph Robert Hamish Deakin (1917–85) was Vicar of St Mary's Church from 1949 to 1973, when he was appointed suffragan Bishop of Tewkesbury. He was born in the Forest of Dean, and after studying at Oxford and Wells Theological College he became a curate in Stroud, then Vicar of Holy Trinity, Drybrook, from 1944 to 1949. The Vicarage for most of his time at St Mary's was on Cirencester Road, near the turning into Bafford Approach, a house now divided into two. There is a 'quiet corner' in St Mary's Churchyard which is dedicated to the memory of Robert Deakin and his wife Marian.

Richard Boroughs, in a photograph taken to mark his completion of seventy years as a member of St Mary's Church choir, 5 June 1941. He had joined the choir on 5 June 1871, when he was nine years old, and he continued in its ranks until 28 March 1948, Easter Sunday, a few days before his death at the age of eighty-six. His funeral service was on 10 April, and in the following month's parish magazine a tribute to him read: 'His record of faithful service in the choir is truly wonderful. . . . His long life spent in the service of the church and the community is an inspiration to us all. Well done thou good and faithful servant. R.I.P.' In his younger days Richard Boroughs had been a member of Ryeworth Cricket Club. A picture of his golden wedding celebration is on page 101.

This picture gives a good view of the 1824 rose window at the west end of St Mary's Church. The window could have been lost at the time of the church restoration of 1878, but the feeling against this was so strong that the architect, John Middleton, instead moved it to its present position and preserved it. The pine pews and the floor tiles date from that time also. The porch was altered, but proved to be so draughty that in about 1886 inner doors of pine with purple bubble glass were installed. These in turn were replaced by the present doors in about 1940. One of the gas standard lights dating from 1878 can be seen on the left, indicating that the photograph dates from before 1914–15, when hanging lights were installed. The monument on the wall to the left of the door is in memory of Sir David Leighton, KCB. He was born in 1774 and died at Bafford House, where he had spent the last thirty-four years of his life. He had previously had a distinguished career in India, including being at the taking of Seringapatam and Jemalabad in 1799, and being for nine years adjutant-general of the Bombay Army. He was typical of the many ex-colonials who retired to Cheltenham and district in the nineteenth century. To the right of the door is a memorial to Samuel Cook, who died in 1804, his nephew Samuel Higgs, who died in 1824, and also in memory of John Gale, who died at Milan, aged twenty-two, in 1829. Cook, Higgs and Gale are names of landowners in Charlton Kings over many years from the eighteenth century.

This delightful picture, taken in the mid-1970s, shows the Vicar of St Mary's at the time, the Revd David Yerburgh, with Miss Annie Hopkins. She was in the process of repainting the railings round the church, a task which she took upon herself. No small undertaking, the exercise attracted a considerable amount of local interest. Annie Hopkins was born in Charlton Kings in 1898, and Elm Cottage in Brevel Terrace was her home nearly all her life. She was a loyal member of St Mary's congregation, and painting the railings was a very practical example of her care for the church. She died in 1986, and her generous bequest to St Mary's was used towards the restoration and extension of the Parish Hall (now St Mary's Parish Centre). One of the meeting rooms in the new upper storey is known as 'Annie's Room', ensuring that she is not forgotten. (Photograph courtesy of the *Gloucestershire Echo*)

The exact date of this photograph is not known, but it was probably taken in about 1900. It shows a caravan belonging to the Church Army, with the officer and, at a guess, a local resident. The caravan appears to be parked on waste ground along Church Street (the east end of St Mary's Church is in the background), and was probably staying in the village for a few days conducting mission services and handing out Christian literature to the local people. The vehicle would probably have been drawn by a horse from place to place during the summer months.

The boys' choir at Holy Apostles' Church, 1876. The choirmaster with them is believed to be Mr Perry, who was the Schoolmaster at Holy Apostles' School. On the extreme left of the picture is F.J. Fry, who later in life became Headmaster of the Boys' School (see page 115). On the extreme right is Frank Bridgman, who in later years wrote a history of Charlton Kings, which (in manuscript) is now held by Cheltenham Local Studies Library. When Holy Apostles' Church was opened, it had a boys' choir, members of whom attended the village school in School Road. The boys had to sing at weekday services on special occasions, causing their absence from school, which was duly noted in the school log book. For instance: '1872: On Wednesday June 7th all the boys who sing in the choir at the New Church were absent, being the anniversary of the opening thereof.' St Mary's boys' choir was started in 1877. By then Holy Apostles' School had opened, so in time choristers for each choir would be likely to be recruited from their local school.

Holy Apostles' Church just after it was completed, 1871. A new church was needed to serve that area of St Mar
parish, and in 1862 Charles Cooke Higgs, who lived at Langton House (now The Langton), gave a piece of his la
at the junction of Cirencester Road and London Road. He also gave £1,000 towards the cost of building a churc
hoping that the rest of the money would be raised by subscriptions. These, however, failed to materialise, a
Mr Higgs eventually paid the full cost of the building, £7,000, himself. The architect engaged was John Middleto
and the foundation stone was laid in March 1866. On completion in 1871 the church was opened by the Bish
of Gloucester, but for the next fourteen years it remained subject to St Mary's and did not have its own clergy.
Mr Higgs tended to behave as though he owned the church (perhaps this was understandable, in t
circumstances), relations between him and the Vicar of St Mary's, the Revd Charles Dundas, were not ea
Meanwhile, in 1872 Holy Apostles' School had been built, again at Mr Higgs's expense, and also a public drinki
fountain which is still there, behind the traffic lights. Charles Cooke Higgs died in 1884. In the following year t
church was formally consecrated and Holy Apostles' became an independent parish.

Opposite: Holy Apostles' Parochial Church Council, August 1948. The Revd Charles Peers, who was Vicar fr
1944 to 1966, is in the centre. Back row, left to right: -?-, -?-, Bob Beekes, -?-, Arthur Mills. Third row: Capta
Everard, Mr Bridgeman, Mr Fuller, -?-, Mr Maude, Miss Castle. Second row: -?-, -?-, -?-, Mrs Dovey, Mavis Adar
Miss Winter, -?-. Front row: Mrs Beresford, Mr Lynes, ?Mrs Lynes, Mr Hawkesford (Vicar's Warden), the Re
Charles Peers, Mrs Peers, Mr Absolon (People's Warden), A. Bridgeman, Mr Birt, Mrs Birt.

The Vicar, Churchwardens, Organist and choir of Holy Apostles' Church, 1919. It was taken to mark the imminent departure of the Vicar, the Revd H.A. Corke, who had been the incumbent since 1904, for the parish of Swindon Village, Cheltenham. Back row, left to right: Mr Timbrell (Sexton), Bailey, A. Mills (Librarian), F. Maisey, ? Corbett, James, -?-. Third row: Mr Tilley, Miss Butler, ? Haslum, Jack Lawrence (Choir Secretary), ? Hill, Miss D.L. Stickley, W. Irving, R. Cook, E. Coldrick, Miss Clifford, Mr Butler. Second row: Mrs Bridgman, Mrs Prothero, Miss Goldfinch, E.L. Ward (Parish Warden), J.C. Williams, LRCM. (Organist and Choirmaster), the Revd H.A. Corke (Vicar), W.H. Symonds (Vicar's Warden), Mrs Birt, Miss Birt, Miss Burnett, ? Walker. Front row: E. Hill, R. Jones, -?-, -?-, -?-, ? Bailey, E. Baxter, ? Denley, B. Baxter, ? Slack. The Parish Warden (now more usually called People's Warden), E.L. Ward, was the owner of the well-known Cheltenham store that bore his name and was situated on the corner of the High Street and North Street where Littlewoods is now. In 1919 he and his family were living at Ashley Rise, Ashley Road, Battledown. The Vicar's Warden, W.H. Symonds, lived in Langton Grove Road and was a jeweller. Arthur Mills, the choir librarian, was a baker in Ryeworth Road. Jack Lawrence, the choir secretary, was a solicitor's clerk. Mrs Birt lived in Ryeworth Road, and her daughter later became Mrs Middleton. The Revd H.A. Corke was succeeded as Vicar of Holy Apostles' by the Revd A.H. Rhodes.

The interior of Holy Apostles' Church as it looked before it was damaged by fire in 1970. This and the next photograph were part of a set taken in the early 1930s for sale, mounted in albums, in aid of a fund to extend the church at the west end to provide vestries. Between the main arches of the nave can be seen carved medallions showing the twelve apostles, and there are also heads of Church Reformation leaders supporting the windows of the north and south aisles.

The font at the west end, with more fine carving to the sides of the west window. Vestries were added here in 1934. The entrance doors were cut through the wall under the window, with steps down from the floor level of the nave. The font was moved, and since the 1970 fire it has been at the east end of the north aisle.

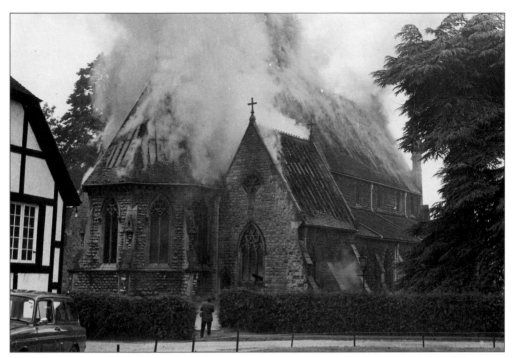

Just after noon on Thursday 18 June 1970 (the day of a General Election), flames could be seen rising to 30 ft above the apex of the roof of Holy Apostles' Church. This dramatic photograph shows the scene. At one time ten fire appliances were fighting the flames, while Holy Apostles' School was evacuated, and London and Cirencester Roads were closed until mid-afternoon. It was later decided that the fire had begun with an electrical fault in the organ. (Photograph courtesy of the *Gloucestershire Echo*)

The Revd Patrick S.M. Walton, Vicar of Holy Apostles', holding the remains of a bible, surveys his church after the fire. The main damage was in the area nearest to the organ, which was a charred ruin, and the organist, Leslie Bloxsome, lost all his own music in addition to the church's. The chancel roof and ceiling were destroyed and some pews were lost, as was the War Memorial Chapel, dedicated in 1948. The windows were mostly spared, as were the registers and the plate. The church was fortunately well insured and repairs were set in hand. Meanwhile the congregation and others rallied round, and services carried on, using the church hall, while a hut behind it was used for the Guides and other organisations. (Photograph courtesy of the *Gloucestershire Echo*)

Exactly two years to the day after the fire which caused such damage, a service of rededication was held at Ho
Apostles' Church. On Saturday 18 June 1972 the Bishop of Gloucester, the Rt Revd Basil Guy, rededicated t
church. This picture of the service in progress gives an indication of the alterations made during the restoratio
A glass screen had been installed, making the chancel into a separate small chapel, and the altar and choir sta
had been brought forward, some damaged pews having been removed. Above them hangs a large cross made
metal. A new Nicholson organ had been installed on the south side of the nave, and John Sanders, Organ
of Gloucester Cathedral, gave an inaugural recital on the new instrument during the following week. Among t
large congregation at the rededication service were the Mayor and Mayoress of Cheltenham, Alderman a
Mrs T.M. Joyner, the Chairman of Charlton Kings UDC, Mr G.H. Hollas and his wife, Canon Robert Deakin, Vic
of St Mary's, Charlton Kings, Canon Evan Hopkins, Rector of Cheltenham, Fr E. McDonnell of Sacred Hearts, a
the Revd Ray Webber of Charlton Kings Baptist church. (Photograph courtesy of the *Gloucestershire Echo*)

Opposite: This picture, taken on 29 June 1957, shows the crowd waiting outside the newly built Sacred Hearts
the arrival of the Bishop of Clifton for the solemn opening of the church. The photograph, taken looking towar
Lyefield Road, shows the west end of the church, which is a light, airy building, seating about 250 people. On t
far side of the west door can be seen a group of the sisters of La Sainte Union. (Photograph courtesy of t
Gloucestershire Echo)

The foundation stone of the Roman Catholic Church of the Sacred Hearts of Jesus and Mary in Moorend Road was laid on 11 February 1956 by the Bishop of Clifton, the Rt Revd Joseph Rudderham. The bishop is seen here blessing the foundations of the building. The Sisters of La Sainte Union had been running the Convent School at Charlton Park since 1939, and services for local Roman Catholics had been held in the school chapel, then later in the school hall, with priests coming from St Gregory's Church, Cheltenham. In 1946 a new Roman Catholic parish was formed and the first priest appointed. The nuns gave the land, and the presbytery was built in 1954, following which plans for the church were drawn up. (Photograph courtesy of the *Gloucestershire Echo*)

John Boyd Rochfort, seen here, came to Charlton Kings in 1865 and began preaching in a house in Moreton Terrace. This small congregation, merely referred to as 'Christian', was the beginning of the Charlton Kings Baptist church. By 1875 the congregation was established enough to buy, with a mortgage, land in Church Street on which William Cleevely was engaged to build a chapel and schoolroom. Rochfort was the pastor, and elders were appointed. In 1887 the question of licensing the chapel for marriages arose: it was thought desirable for the congregation to join an established denomination, and Rochfort recommended alliance with the Baptists. This was agreed, and future people joining (though not existing members) were to be baptised to become Church members. Elders were called deacons from that time. After Rochfort retired in 1888, the church came under some oversight from the pastor of Cambray Baptist church, though it was run mainly by A.W. Ryland until 1932. Since 1938 it has had full-time ministers.

Charlton Kings Baptist church, 1982. From the front it looks as it did when first built, though the building has been extended at the back, where, to celebrate the church's centenary the old schoolroom was replaced in 1975 by a large hall (called the Carey Hall) and another meeting room. The internal layout of the church was also altered. The main door is not used now, the entrance being round the back. The Manse in Grange Walk was also built in 1975.

CHAPTER FOUR

WORK

California Farm (formerly called Hill Farm), July 1952. The traditional farm wagon was still in use at this time, and the horses were still working. Moses Davis, the farmer, was very fond of horses, and he was remembered as one of the last people to ride on horseback round the village about his normal business.

Evidence of the medieval open field system is visible in this picture (taken on 1 January 1978) of
Lower Penny Breaches, seen from Timbercombe Lane. The thin covering of snow makes the lines of
ridge and furrow made by the medieval ploughing more evident.

Holder's Field, at the end of Beeches Road, August 1984, before the remaining perry pear trees had
been removed. The pears, used for making perry, the pear equivalent of cider, grew well in the
heavy clay soil of the vicinity. Much of the so-called cider made in the district was in fact made with
pears, not apples. A few cider presses can still be seen. For example, the one from East End Farm
was restored in 1981 and now stands near the entrance of Balcarras School. For many years in the
1960s and 1970s Holders Field was the setting for the annual Bonfire Night celebration arranged
by the local Scout company. The field takes its name from the Holder family, who formerly owned
the land.

This splendid crop of mangels was the worthy winner of a first prize in an agricultural competition. It was produced at Glenfall Farm some time before 1923, and the farmer, Albert Dowler Mitchell (see page 122) is seen standing alongside, with some of his men in the background. Mangels, also called mangel-wurzels, are grown as food for cattle and sheep.

A traditional farming scene, with free-range poultry, horses and wagon, Old Dole Farm, 1928. The farm became part of the Charlton Park estate in the first half of the nineteenth century and was owned by Sir William Russell, who was by far the largest landowner in Charlton Kings at that time. Later, however, he ran into financial difficulties and had to begin selling off some farms. Others, Old Dole among them, were mortgaged.

This is Starlight, a favourite horse of Moses Davis of Old Dole Farm, painted by George Ryland (see page 77). Early in the Second World War George Ryland was in low spirits, and found solace in long walks with Mr Davis at California Farm. To show his gratitude for the kindness he had received, he painted a picture of Starlight, 'a docile brown gelding that must have stood about 16 hands, with no pretensions to breeding', and by then 'getting on in years'. George Ryland grew up in Charlton Kings, went to the Boys' School, where he first learnt to draw and paint, and later taught at the school, where the work produced by his pupils attracted wide praise. He later taught at Cheltenham Grammar School. He was Scoutmaster, First World War soldier, founder of the Rugby Football Schools' Union, and a keen golfer. His paintings, many of Cotswold scenes, featured in two exhibitions held in the village when he was in his nineties. He died in 1989, aged ninety-seven.

Getting in the harvest at Old Dole Farm, c. 1937. Moses Davis, the farmer, is on the left and Jack Savage is on top of the load. The two young helpers are obviously enjoying the proceedings. The scene is a contrast to modern harvesting, with one man and a combine harvester. The name 'Old Dole' goes back to at least 1557. The farmhouse was rebuilt in 1862–70 by Sir William Russell, to whose estate it then belonged, using stone from a quarry at the west end of Ravensgate Hill. It was bought from his mortgagees at the end of the nineteenth century by Edwin Davis, who was a Cheltenham butcher, for his son Moses. Moses Davis's son and his wife now live at California Farm nearby.

Batten's shop, a licensed grocer's and post office on the corner of London Road and Keynsham Street, late 1920s or early 1930s. It looks a typical 'corner shop' of its time. This is beyond the boundary of Charlton Kings, but the owners seem to have had some links with the village (Batten was a well-known local name for many years in the seventeenth and eighteenth centuries). They advertised local concerts, and, according to the parish magazine, sometimes subscribed to local charitable causes.

This rather faint photograph shows the Copt Elm Road side of the old Gloucester Co-operative Society grocery building (now Smith and Mann), at the junction with Lyefield Road, probably c. 1920. At that time there was another shop door on this side as well as the main doorway, which can just be seen. Above it is a stone stating that this is Branch no. 15 of the Gloucester Co-operative Society, and the date AD 1901. The butcher's section was round the corner in the building now occupied by Magpie: the butcher's tiling can still be seen there. Almost opposite the butcher's, at 2 Lyefield Lawn, Miss Edith Bratt stayed with Mr and Mrs C.H. Jessop, friends of her family, for a year or two just before the First World War. The purpose was to thwart her involvement with the young J.R.R. Tolkien. While in Charlton Kings she would sometimes play the organ at St Mary's or piano solos at church concerts. The separation did not achieve the desired end, and she and Tolkien later married.

This photograph of Cheltenham High Street, decorated for the visit of the Prince of Wales (later Edward VII)
1897, is included because it shows the shop, on the right, belonging to Horace Edwards of Herbert Villa, L
Herberts Road (see page 19). The site, just below the junction with Cambray Place, is now occupied by the Ab
National premises. Horace Edwards inherited from his father the stationer's business founded by his grandfathe
1831. As well as stationery, he sold what his advertisements called 'General Fancy Goods', and printing was d
on the premises too. It was a prosperous business, and Horace Edwards, when living at Herbert Villa, bou
several plots of land on Battledown and later moved there, to a house called Pen Rhys. He was, though, 'in tra
and as such was not listed in the local directories as 'Gentry'. He was a man of strong religious principles a
philanthropic disposition, however, and gave much of his time to church work and social and charitable cau
He was much involved in the setting up of the Charlton Kings Working Men's Club, and served as secretary
treasurer of numerous local committees over a great many years. As well as all this and his generosity to Sun
School children, he also found time to collect newspapers and magazines to take to the inmates of Cheltenh
Workhouse. Such concern for children and the poorest members of society indicates that he was indeed a
gentleman, whatever the directories indicated. Horace Edwards died in 1928 aged eighty-eight; his address at t
time was 10 Pittville Villas, Cheltenham. Next to Horace Edwards' shop is that of Prockter and Forth, chemist
druggist (with its speciality 'Prockter's Carpet Renovator'). Richard Prockter owned land on Battledown for o
thirty years, letting it to farmers, including Jesse Peacey (see page 117). He died in 1896, but the firm contin
trading until at least 1907.

Opposite: Dale's cycle shop, shortly before it closed in 1988. This was the third Dale family shop in Church Str
W. Dale's 'Noted Bacon Shop' had been a few doors further down from here (since demolished), and F. Dale's ra
shop was below Grange Walk. Half of the building on this photograph was originally used by the Charlton Ki
Allotment Society and half by Charles Oram, hairdresser. It is now once more divided into two: half is a solicit
office and half (again) a hairdresser's.

Charlton Kings Fire Brigade was established in 1902, with its base at the UDC's yard in Horsefair Street (where Horsefair Close is now). This photograph was taken shortly after the formation of the brigade. The captain is Mr Harris, though as he lived in Cheltenham Fred Neather (second from left in the back row) was effectively in charge. It is a pity that the men are not pictured wearing their fine decorated brass helmets. When there was a fire the yard foreman would be telephoned, and he would ring the bell to summon the firemen, who were all volunteers. Some men, working out of the village, were reached by bicycle. There was a hand-cart with ladders and a pump and hoses which would be pushed by the men to the sites of rick and chimney fires. It is said that Fred Neather, being a portly man and not able to run as fast as the others, rode on the cart among the ladders. It is not surprising that smaller fires had often been put out by the time the brigade arrived. For a house fire Cheltenham's brigade with its horse-drawn engine would be summoned. The men were paid a retainer of 30s a year, and an extra payment for each fire they attended. One night in 1924 was particularly remembered as there were two fires (and so presumably two payments). After spending much of the night fighting a barn fire at East End Farm, the men stopped on the way home to put out a thatch fire at a cottage behind the Merry Fellow. The brigade was disbanded in 1925 and its duties passed to the Cheltenham service.

A postcard showing Henry G. Woodliffe's chemist's shop on the corner of Hamilton Street on the London Road at Six Ways. The card was posted in August 1910, addressed to Master E. Hull, 1 Britania [*sic*] Road, Great Yarmouth, Norfolk, and reads: 'Dear Eddie, I hope you are quite well. I have sent you a picture of the shop. From Marjorie.' The shop was new in 1910, and as Mr Woodliffe's elder daughter, Marjorie, was then eleven years old, and the card is written in a round, childish hand, it seems more than likely that she was the sender, and the recipient a young cousin or friend. Perhaps the Woodliffes had previously lived in Great Yarmouth, and the reason that they did not remain long (they were not there by 1914) was that they returned to East Anglia. Mr Woodliffe advertises on the window of the shop that he is a 'Graduate in Chemistry and Physic', and states 'Prescriptions Dispensed Accurately'. The public telephone box alongside the shop is of interest. It lists the local code numbers for Cheltenham, Tewkesbury, Cleeve Hill and Bredon. The premises were afterwards for many years a branch of the Midland Bank, subsequently a bathroom and kitchen centre, and are now a complementary health clinic.

Alfred Dyer, undertaker, standing outside his premises in Church Street, 1930s. Alfie Dyer, as he seems to have been generally known, took over the undertaking business from Greville Hamlett. As well as this work the business also made furniture, as indicated over the doorway. The building shown (now Occasions) is at the top of Church Street, just next to the present Infant School car park. The workshop was alongside. Alfred Dyer lived further down Church Street at Conway Cottage, where his cousin Miss Taylor kept house for him (he was unmarried).

An account rendered for a funeral arranged by Alfred Dyer, 1945. The sum charged (£19 10s) may seem extremely modest, but we must take into consideration the fact that wages were very much lower at that time. For example, a junior executive at the Gloucester Railway Carriage and Wagon Company would have earned around £500 per year, so many people would have been paid considerably less than that. The postage stamps, showing George VI's portrait, are affixed in accordance with the law at that time that receipts for over £2 had to be signed over a 2d stamp (or, as here, two penny stamps).

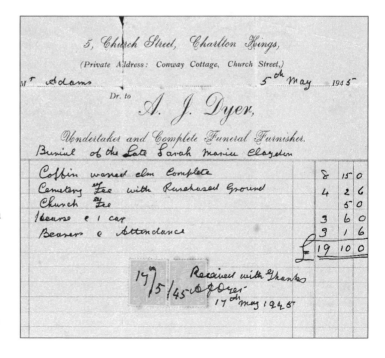

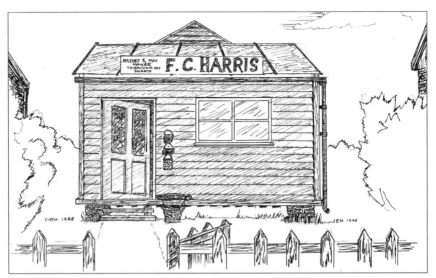

Frederick Harris was born in 1893 in Charlton Kings. He worked in the printing trade, but during service in the First World War he was blinded, and so was admitted to St Dunstan's (a charity founded in 1915 to help war-blinded men and women) to be trained in basket-making and allied crafts. As well as the training, he acquired a wife, who was working as a secretary at St Dunstan's Headquarters. In about 1920, with the help of the charity, Mr Harris took a lease on a plot of land in Lyefield Road West and erected a small wooden lock-up shop selling confectionery, tobacco and cigarettes. In a workshop behind this he made baskets of all types and also coir doormats. This sketch by his son, Ian Harris, shows what the workshop was like.

Fear operated a wireless repair service in the early 1920s from a workshop behind his house, 15 Lyefield Road ...st. Later in the decade he expanded the business, building premises alongside (where Frederick Harris's wooden ...p had been), which are now occupied by Lyefield DIY. His advertisement above dates from the early 1930s, and ...ws examples of old wireless sets among the electrical apparatus. Mr Fear also recharged accumulators, which ...re rather like car batteries, used to power early wirelesses. Mr Fear's public address system was a feature of local ...door events for many years. It is mentioned on the programme for the George V Silver Jubilee Celebrations held ...1935 (see page 104). Mr Fear was also a long-serving leader in the Boy Scout movement (see page 79).

...osite: In the late 1920s, Frederick Harris bought Woodville, the house next door, and converted the front room ...o a tobacconist's shop, also selling confectionery and ceasing the basket-making business. Mr Harris died in ...38, and the following year his widow sold the business and moved with her family to Sandy Lane. Woodville ...ained more or less unchanged until 1998, but was recently slightly altered to give more space inside. It is now ...ost office, also selling cards and stationery.

W. J. & T. H. DYER

Monumental and General Masons

Granite and Marble Memorials to order

Memorials cleaned and kept in order by arrangement . . .

BEST WORK

ESTIMATES AND DESIGNS FREE

Church Street, Charlton Kings

Works : CHURCH STREET

HENDERSON'S
East End Stores
and Post Office

VIEWS of the DISTRICT & CHURCH always in stock

GROCERIES . HABERDASHERY

Agents for LYONS' NOTED CAKES

LONDON ROAD, CHARLTON KINGS

A. J. DYER

UNDERTAKER

Funerals Completely Furnished

5 CHURCH STREET, Charlton Kings

*Private Address—*CONWAY COTTAGE, CHURCH STREET

TELEPHONE - - - - - 2670

G. YOUNG & SON

Motor Engineers

Open and closed Cars for hire.   Day and Night service
WEDDINGS SPECIALLY CATERED FOR
Repairs to any make of car
All Orders receive prompt attention

LYEFIELD GARAGE, LYEFIELD ROAD
CHARLTON KINGS

DOUGLAS H. RYAN

Ladies' and Gentlemen's Tailor

Repairs and Renovations a speciality

OWN MATERIALS MADE UP

Your esteemed patronage is solicited

Glenisla, Copt Elm Road, Charlton Kings

Telephone—CHELTENHAM 3567

A. E. Marshall & Sons

BUILDERS AND DECORATORS

Sanitary Plumbing and Draining
Every kind of Household Repair undertaken
Personal Attention · Estimates Submitted

Fairview, Lyefield Road West, Charlton Kings

F. C. HARRIS
—for—

High - class Chocolates and Sweets
Tobacco and Cigarettes

Brunner's Cakes fresh daily

Large range of Table Delicacies

LYEFIELD ROAD, CHARLTON KINGS

Telephone: Cheltenham 4258

F. C. Skinner

Newsagent and Bookseller

Morning, Evening and Sunday deliveries

CONFECTIONER & TOY DEALER

LENDING LIBRARY

Licensed to sell Tobacco and Cigarettes

The Forge, Church St., Charlton Kings

A. MORRELL

Seedsman and Florist

All kinds of bedding plants in season.
Floral designs made to order at reasonable
prices on the shortest notice . . . .

Cambrian Nursery, Charlton Kings

A selection of advertisements which appeared in a booklet about St Mary's Church by the Revd Edgar Neale in the 1930s. It gives an idea of the range of goods and services available in the village.

CHAPTER FIVE

SCHOOLS

Children and their teacher at Holy Apostles' School, c. 1900. Some of the little girls are wearing the pinafores which were generally worn up to the time of the First World War, and boots are worn by both girls and boys. There was much poverty in Charlton Kings at that time, and this is perhaps apparent in the photograph.

School Road, looking towards Spring Bottom and showing the schools, one on either side of the road. The buildings on the right had been built in 1872, to cater (separately) for boys and girls. When they became inadequate, land on the other side was bought, and the building on the left was built in 1894. The boys moved across the road, the girls moved into the boys' building, and the infants took over the girls' building. Some boys left at eleven to go to the Grammar School (and later girls to Pate's), but most stayed until school-leaving age, and this arrangement continued until 1958 when the new Secondary School in East End Road (later called Balcarras School) was built. The Junior School moved to a site alongside the Secondary School in 1968, leaving the Infants in sole possession of the left-hand-side building (they now have a handsome new building in addition). The premises on the right were sold, the old Infants' School was demolished and the Girls' section remained in use as a supplementary Church Hall for a while before being sold. Now the whole site is used for housing, the development called Old School Mews as a reminder of its history. The School Road Hall Trust educational charity is another reminder, using funds to benefit the education of young people living in Charlton Kings.

e Mandolin Band shown here in 1909 or 1910 was made up of pupils of the Girls' School, who were taught to
ay the mandolin by Miss Daniels in school. There was also a Banjo and Mandolin Band run by Miss Alice
ardiner, who was at one time a teacher at Cheltenham Ladies' College, and it seems likely that some girls would
ave joined that. An old man remembered playing 'dressed as a gypsy' at garden parties and summer fêtes in
aces like Chedworth and Compton Abdale. There was also a group of banjo players about twenty strong known
the Ryeworth Nigger Minstrels.

posite: Boys working at their carpentry at Charlton Kings Boys' School, autumn 1931. The workshop looks well
uipped, and the skills learnt would no doubt prove useful to the boys in the future. There seems to be a wide age
nge, so presumably the tasks were varied accordingly.

Pupils of Charlton Kings Boys' School cultivating the school gardens during the Second World War. The boys are weeding the onion bed under the direction of Mr B. Shorthouse. A variety of vegetables and fruit were produced during the war years – all part of the Dig for Victory campaign to ensure that the country was self-sufficient.

These Charlton Kings Junior School pupils were winners of a recorder group trophy at the Cheltenham Competitive Festival in 1972. Staff standing at the back are, left to right, Mr A. Wilkins (music teacher), Mrs Dilys Robinson, Mr W.S. Ballinger (Headmaster). In the background can be seen the tower of St Mary's Church and the houses on the Glynrosa estate. (Photograph courtesy of the *Gloucestershire Echo*)

Councillor Victor G. Stanton in 1976, the year he served as Mayor of Cheltenham. He is at Charlton Kings County Infants' School in Lyefield Road East, receiving a cheque for £20.85 from Kate Arnold, watched by fellow-pupils. The money was raised from a sponsored swim by children at the school, and it was for the Mayor's charity fund for a day-care centre. As well as his involvement in local politics, Councillor Stanton was the proprietor of Wakefield's grocers in Church Street. After the changes in the village centre, when the supermarket, shops and library were built in the Church Piece precinct, the Stanton Room, the meeting room in the library building, was named after him in recognition of his work in the local community. (Photograph courtesy of the *Gloucestershire Echo*)

This photograph, taken in 1975 or '76 outside one of the buildings of Charlton Kings Infants' School, shows Mrs Lilian Eales being presented with flowers and other gifts in recognition of ten years as a 'lollipop lady'. In this capacity she helped schoolchildren across the busy Church Street/School Road corner, by the Merry Fellow Inn. The picture shows, left to right, Jason Wong, Sarah Randolph, Lawrence Bestwick, Lara Denyer, Mrs Eales, Robbie Auditory, Amy Franklin-Stokes. (Photograph courtesy of the *Gloucestershire Echo*)

A group of pupils at Holy Apostles' School, 1935. Holy Apostles' Church is in the background. Back row, le
right: D. Field, R. Adams, Ken Rose, ? Bishop, Ken Peacey, Roy White, Bill Coombes, Peter Griffin, Bill Phil
Francis Field, Bill Bishop, Norman Mills, R. Mills, Eric Trapp, -?-. Fifth row: Gordon Peacey, Ron Pea
? Appleyard, Peter Appleyard, Norman Buzzard, Colin Woolford, John Philips, ? Mitchell, Jess Gibbons. Fourth r
J. Simms, Jill Boulter, Doreen Smith, Doreen Thatcher, Muriel Gardner, Mavis Adams, Joyce Rose, Phyllis L
Joan Griffiths, Alice Hooper, -?-, Gwen Peacey, Molly Phillips, Eileen Davage, Tony Peacey, Graham Wilkin:
Brian White, David Peacey, -?-, -?-, -?-. Third row: -?-, J. Jennings, Nancy Bethel, Rita Soule, Pam Bethel, M
Ryder, Rachel ?, Barbara Blinkworth, Nancy Rowlands, Diana Freeman, Joan Coombes, Rosie Hooper, M
Rowlands, Nancy Greenman, ? Selley, Marge Fifield, Lois Loud, Irene Pearson, Iris McGregor, Jean Gibbins, -?-,
Trapp twins. Second row: -?-, -?-, Stafford Cooke, Dennis Hooper, -?-, Esme Pearce, -?-, Evelyn Carpenter, -?-, I
Young. Front row: Maurice Haslum, Joyce Field, Margaret Haslum, Vida Mills, Ann Skinner, June Harris, -?-, Da
Field, Dave Walters, -?-, Don Tipper, Tony Apperley, John Drinkwater, Don Drinkwater.

Opposite: St Edward's School's senior pupils now occupy Charlton Park, one of the most significant house
Charlton Kings and seen here in an old print. It was acquired by the Greville family in about 1400, and
timber-framed house built in about 1562 by Giles Greville forms the basis of the present building. John Pr
bought it in 1701, added a brick casing and extended the house. The painting of the house and grounds by
Charlton Kings artist Thomas Robins dating from about 1740 can be seen in Cheltenham Art Gallery
Museum. John Prinn's great granddaughter's husband Dodington Hunt rebuilt the west front and made o
alterations. He entertained George III when the King visited the house in 1788 during his stay in Cheltenh
The grounds, though part sold off for housing, are still spacious, though not as rich in wildlife as shown here.

On 23 July 1966 the foundation stone of the new Holy Apostles' School was laid at its site in Battledown Approach by Mrs Charles Peers, wife of the Vicar of Holy Apostles' Church. This was 100 years after the foundation stone of Holy Apostles' Church had been laid. The original Holy Apostles' School alongside the church dated from 1873–4, and had become unsuitable because of the lack of adequate space and the noise and air pollution caused by the great increase in traffic on the London and Cirencester Roads. The picture shows the foundation stone, which reads: 'This foundation stone was laid by/Mrs Charles Peers/in the centenary year of the Church/July 23rd 1966'. Mr E.J. Emms, the senior trustee of the Charles Cooke Higgs Trust, read out to the parents, pupils and friends present a summary of the year's achievements, written on a scroll which was then put in a copper cylinder and placed behind the foundation stone. Mrs Peers pronounced the stone 'well and truly laid', and the architect, Mr T. Overbury, presented her with the silver trowel as a memento. Left to right: J.R. Sullivan (Headmaster), Canon Charles Peers, K. Mogg (Architect in charge), T. Overbury (Architect), Mrs Peers, E.J. Emms, J.H. Carpenter. (Photograph courtesy of the *Gloucestershire Echo*)

Ashley Manor, which at the time of this photograph (*c.* 1965) was the main building of Whitefriars School, h originally been called Woodlands. It was subsequently renamed Oaklands by Nathaniel Hartland, who ma alterations to the original 1832 building, adding the classic bow window. Sir Frederick Dixon Dixon-Hartla inherited the property in 1877, and in 1888 he changed its name to Ashley Manor. Sir Frederick's widow, La Agnes Dixon-Hartland (see page 40) continued to live there after his death until she herself died in 1955. Aft standing empty for two years the house was bought by the Order of Carmelites and became Whitefriars School, independent secondary school for boys. In 1987 Whitefriars amalgamated with the Convent run by the Sisters La Sainte Union, which was based at Charlton Park, to become the co-educational St Edward's School. The Juni section, together with the Kindergarten, is based at Ashley Manor. New buildings have been added, but t appearance of the main buildings remains as shown here.

CHAPTER SIX

SPORT & LEISURE

*Charlton Kings Rangers football team for 1904/5, after winning a championship trophy.
The only identified player is Horace Marshall, second from the left in the second row. His son
was later to remark that this was the only time he had seen his father without a cigarette in
his mouth!*

Ryeworth Cricket Club's team, probably 1890. George Mitchell, of Ryeworth Farm, is seated in the centre of t
splendid photograph. He had responded to a request in the St Mary's parish magazine for June 1879 for a suita
field so that a parochial cricket club could be set up. Most sporting and social activities in Charlton Kings had th
origins in initiatives of the parish church at that time. To the left of Mr Mitchell, holding a cricket ball, is his s
Albert Dowler Mitchell, who was said by no less a person than W.G. Grace to be a fine bowler. The umpire on
extreme right is John Bate, who died in 1947 aged ninety-one.

Opposite: In 1984 Ryeworth Cricket Club's under-13s won the Cheltenham Knockout Cup, and are pictured h
with their trophy. Their achievement was a tribute to their ability and the work put in by the club in encourag
and coaching the young players. Back row, left to right: Mark Bailey, Martin Sherwood, Chris Rixon. Front ro
J. Jenkins, Chris Townsend, Simon Perry, John Carroll, Dean Vernon. John Carroll went on to play for Cambri
University and Chris Townsend for Oxford.

Ryeworth Cricket Club's 1st XI for the 1952 season. Back row, left to right: N. Staddon (who was Secretary of the club for thirty-six years), J. Blackwell, K. Boulton, A. Brunsdon (Groundsman), B. Newns, R. Stephenson, H. Price. Front row: D. Savage, D. Drinkwater, S. Stubbs (Captain), T. Robjohn, L. Hyde.

A group portrait by J.A. Bailey, showing Holy Apostles' Association Football Club, 1913/14. They were members of Cheltenham and District League (Division 3). It states that they had played 22 matches, won 15, lost 5 and drawn 2, so they had had a satisfactory season. By the following season the First World War would have meant great changes. Back row, left to right: A.J.W. Stickley, F. Bridgman, J. Davey, C.H. Dickins, A. Powell, H.H. Fry, H. Bate, H. Wheeler, E.T. Searle, F. Satchell. Middle row: W. Davey, E.J. Burrows, F.H. Taylor (Hon. Secretary and Treasurer), L. Hart (Captain), H.G. Davey (Vice-Captain), J.O. Lewis, E. Griffiths. Front row: A. Roberts, F.J. Scrivens, W.J. Chandler. Mr Stickley can also be seen on page 102.

A similar photograph, but showing Charlton Kings Association Football Club for the season 1911/12, when they won the Cheltenham League Division 3. The trophy is proudly displayed in front of the captain. Back row, left to right: S.C. Nash, C. Lewis, T. Coomby, H. White, R. Masters, A. Hughes, B. Bloodworth, R. Reid, W. Butler (Hon. Secretary). Middle row: W. Hancock, P. Bush, R. Smith, A. Boroughs (Captain), D. Mobley, H. Burrows (Vice-Captain), P. Strickland. Front row: H. Bendall, H. Smith.

Lilleybrook Golf Club was founded in 1922, the year in which Lilleybrook House became a hotel, after the departure of the Lord family. A new clubhouse was built in the early 1970s, but was replaced by the present building in 1986. This photograph was taken on President's Day, 1965. George Ryland (see pages 34 and 56), who was Club Secretary at the time, is on the extreme left of the front row. Also in the front row, left to right, are: Mrs M. Campbell, Mrs V. Spencer-Cox, Mrs Taylor (Mayoress of Cheltenham), Ian McLennan, Miss Craig (Ladies' Captain), Bertram Taylor (Mayor of Cheltenham), K. Cooke (Club President), Bill Allen, Mrs L. Cook, G. Shenton. The picture also shows T. Field, E. Walker, Judith Millican, F. Stephens, F.A. Carey, Miss Townsend, P. Baker, D. McLennan, Val Shorey, M. Barkas, I. Grainger, B. Moore, M. Ryland, M. Brown, J. Bramwell, E. Shenton, I. Dodsworth, R. Millard, T. Bailey, J. Miles, R.L. Bramwell, Topper Brown, J. Baker, P.K. Carter, Roy Allen, B. Callaghan, J. Miller, R. Johnson, R. Jessop, G. Paton, D. Moore, D. Evans, D. Price, R. Bevan, R. Shorey and R. Peacey.

The Cotswold Hounds with Lilleybrook House in the background, 1906. The Hunt, of which H.O. Lord was the Master, would often meet at Lilleybrook during the time the Lords lived there, and it was a familiar sight in the local countryside. An old man, who was a boy at the time, remarked that 'Mr Lord used to rave and swear terrible when hunting'.

These decorated bicycles were photographed at an annual flower and horticultural show in the grounds of Lilleybrook House, probably before the First World War, while the estate was owned by the Lords. Mrs Lord was particularly interested in farming and horticulture, while her husband's main interest was hunting. The annual show was a great village day out, and the competitions attracted many entries. There were also roundabouts, coconut shies, athletics, various displays and usually a regimental band.

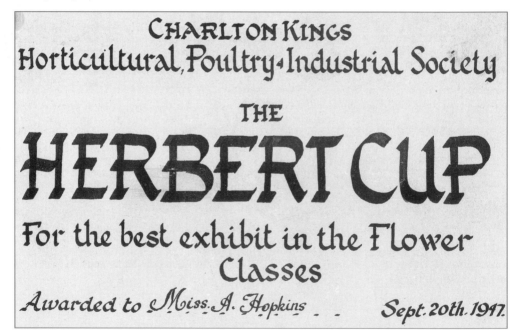

This certificate records that the Herbert Cup for the best exhibition in the flower classes at the Charlton Kings Horticultural Show on 20 September 1947 was awarded to Miss Annie Hopkins. She must have inherited her love and knowledge of flowers from her father, Thomas Hopkins, who was a professional gardener. The Horticultural Society ran an annual flower and vegetable show, which by 1947 was held on Cox's Meadow, Old Bath Road, Cheltenham. The event was a popular one, and many entrants strove for the coveted trophies and prizes.

A group of the Charlton Kings Scouts in the grounds of Moorend Park, 1922. The occasion is probably some sort of jamboree. Back row, left to right: J. Humphries, ? Hancock, E.J. Fear. Fifth row: L. Hancock, B. Gardiner. Handstands: J. Sealey, ? Burrows, ? Wheeler. Bar: -?-, ? Perris, ? Mills, -?-. Fourth row: H. Jeans, H. Evans, ?. Lawrence, P. Bridgman, ? Lawrence, ? Crockshall, ? Short. Third row: ? Peacey, J. Peacey, B. Hughes, ? Sealey, ?. Laurence. Second row: R. Peacey, B. Brunsden, R. Rickards, L. Eaketts, R. Bunce, ? Merrett, Pat Cooper, George Rickards, -?-, Harold Cook. Front row: D. Mustoe, D. Eaketts, B. Eaketts, Jerry Protherough. The Scoutmaster, standing on the left, is J.J. Thorn, who in 1923 succeeded F.J.Fry as headmaster of the Boys' School in Charlton Kings. In 1925 Mr Thorn was followed as Scoutmaster by Ken Cleevely, seen in the picture as Assistant Scoutmaster, on the right. Later E.J. Fear, in the back row above, became Scoutmaster and was a leading figure in the Scout movement in the county for many years. During the First World War, apart from usual scouting activities, the Scouts learnt first aid, stretcher drill and rifle shooting, and helped at Moorend Park which was being used as a war hospital, qualifying for a War Service Badge after a specified number of hours of work. During the Second World War Scouts distributed gas masks, collected waste paper, books and magazines, and ran messages for Air Raid Wardens.

A Girl Guide camp, 1915. The four Guides at Lineover Wood are probably gathering wood for their camp fire. It is interesting to note the changes in uniform that have taken place since 1915. The Girl Guide Movement was established in 1910, following the successful launching of Baden-Powell's Boy Scouts in 1908. The present Charlton Kings Guide Company began in 1952.

The Sea Rangers (SRS *Bellerophon*), who were based at Holy Apostles' Church Hall, *c.* 1944. They are shown assembled outside Cheltenham Ladies' College taking part in a parade. They certainly look extremely smart and well drilled. Being so far from the sea must have been a drawback for such an organisation, but it would have been a good training for those who wanted to join the WRNS. Practical training took place at Tewkesbury.

e Junior Training Corps of Company 900, St Mary's, arlton Kings, of the Church Lads' Brigade at their nual Inspection, held on the Beeches playing field, 56. In 1896 the Revd Thomas Hodson stated that hoped to start a Church Lads' Brigade. He had a ilitary friend who has offered to help in drilling em', and asked for other help. By December of that ar Captain Gray had reported that 'the lads were ing well' and 'becoming more amenable', though the ar would have liked more parental encouragement. e first church parade was held in January 1897, en the boys 'received much favourable comment m the members of the congregation'. An outing to urchdown Hill in September 1897, with 'a meat tea' d cricket match, was much enjoyed. All was not ng entirely smoothly, though, and there was viously an unruly element, since we read in January 98 that the Church Lads' Brigade had 'for the sent ceased to exist'. A few troublemakers had been noved, and had caused difficulties which led to the solution. In December of the same year, however, e Brigade was able to resume, and continued to urish. The Church Lads' Brigade in Charlton Kings ally closed in the mid-1970s.

The 1st Charlton Kings Company of the Boys' Brigade, summer 1944. The Boys' Brigade is an interdenominational body, which was founded in Glasgow in 1883. In Gloucestershire there are fifteen companies, of which the 1st Charlton Kings Company is the oldest: it was founded in May 1942 at Charlton Kings Baptist church by David Harding. The band was formed by Ted Mitchell. Back row, left to right: Lieutenant Ted Mitchell, Ron Phillips, Ken Drake (drum major), Ken Lines, David Jones, -?-, Colour Sergeant Claude Fowler, Sergeant Cyril Herbert, Don Drake, Norman Forest, -?-, Michael James, John Hall, -?-, Jerry Wilkinson, the Revd Hugh Lloyd (Baptist Minister, 1938–46), Captain David Harding, Ken White. Front row: George Williams, Bill Duguid, Keith Wilkinson, Ken Martin, Len Flack, Ian Duguid, Eddie Bateman, Trevor Bond, Harry Nicholas, -?-, Tony Lines.

A group of Girls' Brigade (Juniors) members, at a display in 1981. The Revd Hugh Lloyd's wife formed a company of the Girls' Brigade at about the same time as her husband founded the Boys' Brigade Company. It must have lapsed after the Lloyds left in 1946, though, for in the pamphlet published for the Baptist church's centenary in 1975 it states that in February 1959 the company was re-formed and was affiliated in September of that year. Left to right: Jayne Brookes, Mrs Eileen Reed (officer), -?-, Sarah Martin, Lucy Tyler, Elaine Fennell, Samantha Payne, Vicki Williams, Victoria Ayrton.

The Girls' Friendly Society caravan, which presumably travelled from place to place with material about the organisation, helping members of the various branches to keep in touch with the society. It was recalled by Annie Hopkins as having visited Charlton Kings once when she was a member. She joined in 1913 and remained a member until at least 1920 and probably longer. She said the caravan 'came to the recreation ground in Lyefield Road (now part of the school playground)'. She went on to remark that she had had 'nice holidays with the GFS', and 'couldn't have gone to half the places I did' if it hadn't been for the organisation. The reference to Princess Mary is presumably to the future Princess Royal, daughter of King George V and Queen Mary, and sister of King George VI, who in 1922 married Viscount Lascelles (later the Earl of Harewood). She was probably patron of the GFS.

We do not know the exact occasion of this photograph, but it shows Fred Harris and his band playing a waltz for a local dance in the 1930s. The banjo player's identity is unfortunately unknown, but the drums are played by Fred Harris himself, who owned the tobacconist's shop shown on page 62. Reg Hancock is playing the violin and Fred Cox the piano (complete with candleholders on the front). The band played locally, often at the St Clair Ford Hall of the Working Men's Club, and in many villages in the Cotswolds as well as for servants' dances at houses like Stowell Park, near Northleach. If a larger band was needed for a particular event, extra players would be engaged, increasing the band to eight or ten in number. Both Fred Harris and Fred Cox had previously played in George Maisey's Band. Fred Cox also played the organ at St Mary's Church in the early 1930s. He served in the Second World War, in the Medical Corps and Regimental Band of the Gloucestershire Regiment (as did George Maisey). After the war he worked for the Gloucester Aircraft Company.

George Maisey acting as Master of Ceremonies at a St Mary's parish Christmas party at the Pittville Pump Room, Cheltenham, probably 1970s. For many years this was a popular annual social event for people of all ages. Mr Maisey, who lived in Gladstone Road, was well known locally for his dance band, which was in demand for social events in the Cheltenham area. On his death he left a generous legacy to St Mary's Church, which helped to pay for the restructuring of the Parish Hall, completed in 1985.

Miss Ethel Gwendoline Berkeley (known as 'Gwennie'), the elder daughter of the Revd and Mrs W.N. Berkeley of Charlton Lawn, 1913. She is in the Russian costume she wore when performing in the balalaika orchestra run by Miss Alice Gardiner. The balalaika orchestra gave concerts in aid of various good causes. The Berkeley family – there was also a younger daughter, Muriel May – said to be related to the Berkeleys of Berkeley Castle, came to live at Charlton Lawn in 1896. This is the large house at the top of Copt Elm Road, on the corner with Cudnall Street, now divided into flats. Miss Berkeley was a keen musician, and was also interested in photography. She had her own dark room for developing photographs, among them the one shown here. She and her sister served as VAD nurses during the First World War, at The Priory in London Road, Cheltenham. Miss Berkeley remained unmarried. In 1945, after the deaths of her parents in their nineties, she went to live in Leckhampton Road, where she was later joined by her sister and brother-in-law after they were forced to flee from Egypt after the Suez crisis. Gwendoline Berkeley died in October 1956, aged seventy-seven.

Charlton Kings Community Players was set up in 1992. Membership is from the churches and from those who are resident in or who have strong connections with Charlton Kings, and members cover a wide age-range. Pictured here are some members of the cast of *The Sound of Music*, which was performed in 1998. Kate Nye and Martyn Fry are seen with the children, left to right: Hannah Maynard, Isabel Powell, Rebecca Holder, Georgina Lewis, Gavin Irvine, Emma Cleveland, Tom Clancy. The photograph was taken in the hall of Cowley Manor. Among previous productions are *Toad of Toad Hall*, *The Vigil* and *An Inspector Calls*. Members of the group have, among other things, given entertainments for old people's homes and contributed to outdoor ecumenical events. Over £9,000 has been raised for local good causes such as Balcarras School library, the Old People's Minibus Appeal and Delancey Hospital's League of Friends.

There are now three branches of the Women's Institute in Charlton Kings, the first having been inaugurated on 2 March 1970, when over seventy members gathered at Holy Apostles' Hall and Mrs Irene Mills became the first president. At present, in addition to this branch, there is the Village WI, which meets in St Mary's Parish Centre (both of these have evening meetings), and an Afternoon WI. This photograph shows representatives of the three planting a tree in the precinct outside Charlton Kings Library on 23 February 1978 to mark (rather late!) the Silver Jubilee of 1977. The lady on the left of the three planters is Mrs Phyllis Drinkwater, the 1977 president of Charlton Kings WI, together with representatives of the Village and the Six Ways Afternoon WIs. Among the spectators are Mrs Marie Aston, Mrs Joan Whiteman, Mrs Woodward, Mrs Shipley and Miss Edith Mason. (Photograph courtesy of the *Gloucestershire Echo*)

Members of Charlton Kings Choral Society at a social event, 1960s. Back row, left to right: the Revd W. Watts, Laurence Hudson, Ron Smith (conductor), the Revd Robert Deakin, Tony Hewitt-Jones, Alan Franklin. Front row: Mrs W. Watts, Mrs Pridgeon, Mrs Marjorie Hooper, Mrs Annie Hawkins, Mrs Doreen Munday, Alfred Briggs.

A group picture of Charlton Kings Choral Society, 1995. The conductor, John Wright, is in the middle, and the accompanist, Peter Meason, seventh from the left of the men in the back row. The present choral society was formed in 1957 by a group of villagers led by the Revd Robert Deakin, the Vicar of St Mary's Church at the time. Charlton Kings Choral Society had, however, existed before. It seems to have had its origin when the then Vicar, the Revd Thomas Hodson, announced in St Mary's parish magazine of November 1895 that Mr Brasher, the organist, would be starting an 'Elementary Class for Singing and Music' on Wednesday 20 November. There is no further mention of classes, but the next month's magazine announces that the 'Choral Society' will meet on Monday 2 December at 7.45 pm in the St Clair Ford Hall. The next reference to it is in February 1896, when we read that 'Our Choral Society under Mr Brasher's conductorship is doing admirable work'. By January 1897 the society was 'fast becoming an important fact in our parish, and believes not only in good music but in a good cup of tea'! In September of that year, after the summer break, the forthcoming rehearsals were to be for two concerts, performing Van Bree's *St Cecilia's Day* (along with a 'Miscellaneous Selection'), and Gaul's *Holy City* – both works which now seem to have sunk without trace. The fee for the entire season was given as 2s, not including music. There were apparently preliminary classes for those with 'good voices but possessing no knowledge of music'. At some stage an orchestral section was also established, and concerts continued to be held regularly until at least the 1920s. It is not known why this first phase of the choral society was discontinued. Since its refounding, however, it has continued to flourish, and it now numbers about 120 members.

The Working Men's Club is seen here on a postcard sent in October 1906. It is a handsome building, and a great asset to the life of the village, even more so at the time when people tended to go less far afield in their leisure time and there were few other premises available for societies and activities. The appearance of the building is not greatly changed now, but it has lost its gate-posts and railings, and its distinctive windows have been exchanged for rather bland aluminium double-glazing (done, unfortunately, before this part of the village was designated a conservation area). The sundial on the side of the base of the decorative cupola (not visible in this picture) has now gone, the decorative plasterwork is no longer picked out in a darker colour and the entrance notice to the St Clair Ford Hall is no longer there. The hanging sign has been taken down, and there is now a flagpole above the doorway. The club is still very busy and popular, but the facilities offered no longer include a reading room, chess club, gymnasium, art classes or rifle range.

The Ryeworth Inn, decorated for the Silver Jubilee of Queen Elizabeth II, 1977. In the 1930s the landlord, Mr Fowler, kept a monkey in a cage in the garden. It was from the Ryeworth Inn that the Whit Monday walking races began (see page 105). The garden has now made way for a car park.

The London Inn, on the London Road at Six Ways, was built in the early 1830s by Sampson Mitchell, innkeeper. That stretch of the London Road had been cut through in 1825–6, and from the inn's foundation it was patronised by travellers as well as local people, as it still is. From 1868 until the early 1920s it was the venue of the Ashley Manor courts. This picture, from a pastel drawing by K.S. Preston, shows the inn possibly in the 1950s. The side of the building in Oakland Street has since been altered, but the bracket where the telephone wires were fixed is still there.

The London Inn in more recent years. It is much brighter, offers its customers more, and has for some years been notable for its floral decorations. Each summer its frontage is a mass of flowers, and it has won many awards in the 'Cheltenham in Bloom' competition. This photograph shows the inn in its floral splendour.

CHAPTER SEVEN

TRANSPORT

Two methods of transport – a small pram in the background and a large horse on to which the child is being lifted. The photograph shows Moses Davis, of Old Dole Farm, with part of the farmhouse in the background and his son Bob; it was taken in about 1933.

Moses Davis and his young son Bob at Old Dole Farm, riding on the farm wagon on which the name DAVIS is painted, *c.* 1935. These wagons were a characteristic of farms in the days before agriculture was mechanised, the designs varying in different parts of the country.

A handsome motor-cycle combination, photographed by J.A. Williams of Charlton Kings. The lady sitting on the machine does not seem to be dressed for serious motor-cycling, so she is probably just posing for the photographer. The number AD507 was first issued, on 20 May 1905, to Mr Egerton Cripps of Stratton Firs, Cirencester, with the machine described simply as 'motor bicycle'. That registration was later made void, and the number was re-used on 5 March 1915 for a 'Triumph, 1914, one cylinder, 3½ HP', registered in the name of George Archibald Walker, London Road, Charlton Kings. He owned the machine until June 1920, so it seems most likely that the photograph was taken during the time of his ownership. We do not know who George Archibald Walker was – he is not listed as a householder – but he could have been a member of the family of E. Walker, who owned the baker's and corn chandler's on London Road at Six Ways (see page 9).

r Griffiths was a coal merchant, whose yard, at the beginning of the twentieth century, was near that of the
dertaker's business in Church Street owned by Greville Hamlett and later by Alfred Dyer (see page 61). The
cture, dating from about 1900, shows presumably Mr Griffiths, who is most likely to be in front by the horse,
d his staff, together with two children and a dog. Unfortunately we have no definite identifications. There were
any more coal merchants in the years before gas, electric and oil heating.

Charlton Kings station looking east, i.e. away from Cheltenham, 1909. The photograph was taken from beyond the end of the platform and shows the signal box, with the signalman looking out. Other railway staff are on the platform. The station was obviously kept very neat and tidy, with well-tended flowers and shrubs.

Another view of the station, also looking east and taken at roughly the same time, but nearer the bridge and with a locomotive on the line. The houses on the left of the picture are on Cirencester Road, which crosses the railway at the bridge. The houses with timbered gables are the pair known as The Pines. Nowadays the view from the houses is of Charlton Kings Industrial Estate, which was built on the station site, though this is partly screened by the trees which have grown up since the time of the photograph.

A railway locomotive on the Kingham Line running behind gardens in Ravensgate Road, 1956. The first train steamed into Charlton Kings station in 1881, but the real glory days were from 1899. From then until 1914 there were local trains to Cheltenham, Banbury and Swindon; major expresses passed through, and would stop if the guard had been advised beforehand. It was possible, therefore, to travel widely from the station, which was fully staffed. In the First World War the station was of great strategic importance, and thousands of men passed through on their way to the continent. In the other direction many casualties were transported to military hospitals. After the war the line's importance diminished, but the Second World War brought increased use again, with many troops and munitions being carried and, again, casualties to military hospitals. After the Second World War the use of the line declined, and freight facilities were lost from 1954. From April 1956 the station was reduced to a halt, and finally the line was closed in 1962. The track was taken up two or three years afterwards. At the time when this photograph was taken the houses in Ravensgate Road were being built, and one can see the garden plots marked out. Some years after the track was taken up the owners of the houses were able to purchase the section of cutting behind their properties to extend their gardens. Part of the cutting near the Little Herberts Road railway bridge has been made into a nature reserve.

On this photograph, taken at the same point, the line can be clearly seen, and also a railway hut on the bank. The countryside beyond the line remains much as shown here, and it is hoped that it will continue to do so.

This postcard, postmarked 20 December 1907, shows part of Cirencester Road, with the junction with Pumphreys Road on the right. Electric trams came to Charlton Kings in 1903, and the one seen here was on its way to the terminus at the New Inn (now the Little Owl). Apart from the tram and a couple of bicycles, the road is traffic free. This is probably the most striking difference from the equivalent view nowadays, when nobody would suggest that children (or anyone) should stand in the road to be photographed. The left-hand side of the road has not yet been built up. The houses on the right look much as they do now, though they all still have their front walls intact, this being before the era of car ownership.

A good view of a tram nearly at the top of Copt Elm Road, c. 1910. The overhead wires can be seen, as can the curve of the tram staircase, the driver, and someone leaning over the rail surrounding the open upper deck. The destination board reads 'Charlton Kings', and John Lance & Co. (a large store in Cheltenham High Street, the forerunner of Shirer's and Lance's, which lasted until the later 1970s) is advertised on the front. The Co-op building can be seen on the extreme left. The man standing to the left of the tram is probably a road-sweeper. The trees have now been replaced by smaller, ornamental trees, as can be seen in the lower picture on page 12. The original of this photograph is a postcard which is postmarked 3.15 am, 25 December. The year is indistinct, but the date and time give an indication of the long hours and short holidays at the beginning of the century.

The couple in this splendid vehicle, which is most probably a 1908–9 Rover, photographed in 1909, are Dr Richard Davies and his wife, Dorothy Kathleen (née Lane). Dr Davies was born in Hereford in 1866, received his medical training at Edinburgh University and moved to Cheltenham General Hospital in 1894. In addition to his medical work Dr Davies was active in local politics and was a Cheltenham borough councillor (1899–1911), an alderman (1914–19), and Gloucestershire county councillor (1922–5). In the 1918 General Election he stood as Liberal Coalition candidate for Charlton Kings (see page 118). Dr Davies lived at Glendower, Oakley Road, Battledown, from 1919 until 1930.

Mr and Mrs R.J. Webb are seen here on their way, in costume, to the Cheltenham Pageant of 1908. In 1897 a new company, Webb Brothers Ltd, was formed at Battledown, Roland J. Webb and his brother Harold having bought the Battledown Brick and Terra Cotta Company. Roland became the first managing director. He was, as were most of his family, an enthusiast for sport, particularly tennis and golf. He was also a keen motorist in the early days of motoring, and his garage had a pit where he could undertake repairs. Among his many other interests were chess and photography (he had his own darkroom), and he travelled widely. His wife, Lilian, was a good golfer. She also took an active part in local amateur dramatics.

Master Bob Davis at the wheel of the Bullnose Morris belonging to his father, Moses Davis of Old Dole Farm, *c.* 1936. Though horses were still being used on the farm at that time, the internal combustion engine was beginning to make its impact.

A Black and White Motorways coach (a Gilford) at the Charlton Kings depot, which was on the Cirencester Road at the junction with Bafford Lane/Newcourt Road, *c.* 1928. In July 1926 George Readings, the founder of Black and White, began running short tours round Cheltenham. His first vehicle was a fourteen-seater Reo, but he already had two twenty-seater coaches on order, intending to run a service between Cheltenham and London. This began in November 1926 and was a great success. Although there was by law a 12 mph speed limit, the coach managed to reach London in about four hours, including a refreshment break in Oxford. The original advertisement for the Cheltenham to London service gives the fare as 8*s* 6*d* single and 14*s* for an eight-day return. The coach left Cambray at 8.45 am, and left London at 2 pm. Seats had to be bought in advance (the Charlton Kings ticket agency was C.H. Beard's grocer's on London Road), and passengers were allowed only one suitcase each. The head office was at 411 High Street, Cheltenham, and the garage at Charlton Kings, until the firm expanded. As more vehicles were acquired two and then three services per day and a Sunday service were added. By the beginning of 1928 services were expanding, and Cheltenham was set to become the hub of a nationwide coach system.

CHAPTER EIGHT

SPECIAL OCCASIONS

*his delightful picture is something of a mystery. It was obviously taken very early in the twentieth century,
rhaps 1910–12 from the evidence of the clothing. Woodward's coal cart has been cleaned and the horse has
brasses and flowers on its harness. A boy on the front of the cart appears to be dressed as a jester, and the
oster on the horse's collar reads 'MATHIAS', though the 'S' is very faint. The children might be about to go
 some sort of 'treat'. The Revd Edgar Neale used to enlist the help of various tradesmen in taking children to
Sunday School treats, such as were held at Herbert Villa (see page 19).*

The St Clair Ford Hall was a popular venue for wedding receptions, and this photograph, taken in the 192_ shows what must have been a typical village wedding group of the time.

group of Charlton Kings UDC employees at Charlton Kings station, about to set off on their annual outing to St
iles's Fair at Oxford, 1912. The fair is still held, on a Monday in September. It had become very popular in
ictorian times, when trains brought visitors from as far away as Wolverhampton and Cardiff. It had been a pretty
owdy affair, but later became better policed and more civilised, though still a good day out. Two women and two
hildren have been included in the photograph, but they have probably come to see the party leave on the train.
ll the men look very smart for their day out, with a good variety of headgear. Flat caps are slightly in the
ajority, though five are resplendent in boaters and one is very dapper in his bowler. Back row, left to right
mitting women and children): F. Neather, Fred Pearce, -?-, ? Aylin, -?-, ? Hicks, -?-. ? Harris, ? James, -?-, -?-,
/. Peacey, ? Searson, Frank Timbrell, ? James, Sid 'Soldier' Smith, ? Isher, Horace Matthews. Front row: -?-,
Harris, J. White, -?-, ? Harris, Bob Hamlin, Billy Herbert.

posite: On Monday 5 January 1914 a party of women and children of Charlton Kings, very likely the families of
embers of the Working Men's Club, were entertained to tea at the St Clair Ford Hall, and this picture shows the
casion, giving some idea of the interior of the hall. The Christmas decorations are in place, and the hall was the
nue for many parties and other such events over the Christmas season. The parish magazine mentions the choir
pper, the choirboys' party, and the annual social of the Guilds, and there would have been other events too.
ost of these depended on the generosity and practical help of the better-off inhabitants, and their efforts must
ve brought great pleasure to many whose day-to-day lives were hard, and whose 'treats' were few. The Revd
H. Bouth and his wife, in the foreground of the picture, lived at Battledown Court from 1915 to 1940 (see also
ge 104), and Mr C.L. Grundy, on the right, lived at East Court. He was a member of St Mary's Church Council,
d he and his wife were active in supporting good causes, their names figuring in many subscription lists.

An outing about to depart from the front of the New Inn, probably 1922. The pub is now called the Little Owl i honour of the winner of the 1981 Cheltenham Gold Cup owned by local man Jim Wilson. The occasion an destination are unknown, but the group may be members of a men's organisation, or they may be employees the UDC. The children may be only present for the photograph. The little girl fifth from the left in the front row Dorothy Eaketts, the daughter of G.M. Eaketts, the landlord of the New Inn, who is to the right of her. The oth little girl is Patricia Brookes, whose father is standing by the windscreen of the coach. Almost all the many loc organisations had outings in charabancs in the 1920s, when private car ownership was still rare. With solid tyr and cart-spring suspension, the vehicles cannot have been comfortable by modern standards, but they gave ma an opportunity to see places such as Tewkesbury, Malvern, Oxford and Stratford-upon-Avon, all popul destinations for outings.

Opposite: This group of 'Ancient Britons' consists of Battledown Tilemakers, employees of Webb Brothers, who to part in the great Cheltenham Pageant of 1908. In its literature the firm proclaimed that brick-making in t Battledown area had been started in AD 836 by King Alfred. Thus for this occasion Harold Webb was rath anachronistically dressed in skins as King Alfred. In Cheltenham High Street he halted his men outside a ba and presented a cheque drawn on a roll of sackcloth to pay their wages.

and Mrs Richard Boroughs celebrated their golden wedding in 1935 with a party for members of the Mothers'
ion at their home in Mansfield Place, Horsefair Street (this is the row of houses near the Lyefield Road end of
orsefair Street, opposite Pound Walk). Richard Boroughs, a carpenter, had married Alice Miriam Peacey at St
ary's Church on 8 June 1885, when he was twenty-three. His bride, who was twenty-two, was the daughter of
se Peacey, timber merchant (see page 117). The couple are seated in the middle, behind a tea trolley with a
tted plant on it, presumably gifts which have been presented on behalf of the assembled MU members. The
car, the Revd Edgar Neale, is sitting to the left of Mr Boroughs. Third from left in the back row is Mrs Millicent
ith, who died in 1998 aged 100 years. Mr Boroughs was a long-serving member of St Mary's Church choir
e page 43).

This photograph was taken after the marriage of Alfred J.W. Stickley and Miss Rooke at Holy Apostles' Church, 1897. The bridegroom had come on visits from Birmingham earlier in the 1890s, in connection with his auditing work. It was his custom to stay at the Pierpoint Hotel in Royal Well, which Miss Rooke helped her sister to run. At that time it was not as customary for brides to wear white dresses and veils as it became later, and an elaborately trimmed dress and hat, as here, were more usual. After their marriage the couple lived in Langton Grove Road. They had a daughter, Dorothy.

Following his first wife's death Mr Stickley married for a second time, in 1922, again at Holy Apostles' Church. This time his bride was Miss Constance Ellison, whose father, a manufacturing chemist, had moved to Cheltenham from Boot's of Nottingham to work for the Cheltenham chemists' company UCAL. This photograph was taken after the wedding at Lyefield Villas, Copt Elm Road, and seems to be a simpler occasion, as one would expect for a second marriage. There was a son of this marriage, who later married the daughter of the couple whose wedding picture is at top of the next page.

This wedding group was photographed in 1922, following the marriage at Holy Apostles' Church of Lizzie May Birt, of Elmore, Ryeworth Road, and Charles Middleton. The picture was taken in the garden at The Chase, East End, the home of Mr Harris, the bridegroom's grandfather. Both the bride and her mother were members of Holy Apostles' choir (see page 47), and her father, H. Birt, served as churchwarden there.

Another example of wedding fashions. This group was photographed after the marriage, in February 1926, of Judith Joan Ward and Charles Williams. The bride was the younger daughter of Mr and Mrs E.L. Ward. Mr Ward was the owner of the store bearing his name that stood on the corner of High Street and North Street, Cheltenham, where Littlewoods is now. From 1916 until 1921 the Wards lived on Battledown, and Edward Ward was a trustee of the estate from 1919 until he moved elsewhere in 1921. He continued to serve as a churchwarden of Holy Apostles' Church until 1926, and Judith's wedding took place there, though the Wards were by then living in Toddington. Back row, left to right: C. Wright, Charles Williams, Judith Joan Williams, Barbara Ward, Edward L. Ward. Seated: Mrs Williams, Mrs Ward.

PROGRAMME

Prior to the opening of the Celebrations in Charlton Park, a Thanksgiving Service will be held at St. Mary's Parish Church at 10.30 a.m.

2 p.m.	OPENING CEREMONY.
	National Anthem and breaking of the Flag.
	Short address by Rev. R. H. M. Booth, M.A., J.P., introduced by Mr. W. S. F. Harris, Chairman of Charlton Kings Urban District Council.
	The flag will be broken by the Charlton Kings Troup of Boy Scouts, supported by the Holy Apostles' Company of Girl Guides.
2.15 p.m.	Children's Sports.
4.15 p.m.	Children's Tea.
5.15 p.m.	Children's Sports (continued).
7.40 p.m.	Greetings to the King from the Empire broadcast by loudspeaker.
8 p.m.	His Majesty's Jubilee Speech to the Empire, broadcast by loudspeaker.
8.10 p.m.	Adult Races.
8.15 p.m.	Presentation of Prizes. Dancing on the Green. All the Fun of the Fair.

ALL THE FUN OF THE FAIR

During the afternoon and evening side shows available include :—

Bowling for Live Pig (Pig kindly presented by Mr. S. Shenton)	
Miniature Golf.	Coconut Shies
Spot the Stars	Roll the Penny
Table Skittles	Darts
Pin Table Bagatelle	Treasure Hunt
Ring Games	Lawn Skittles
Bowls	etc., etc.

Prizes of cigarettes or chocolates will be offered in most of the above.
Teas and refreshments for adults will be available at Popular Prices.
Music during the afternoon and evening will be provided by Radio-Gram arranged by Mr. E. J. Fear.

PROGRAMME OF SPORTS EVENTS
open to Children of Charlton Kings

SECTION A.—Open to Juniors and Infants attending the Elementary Schools in Charlton Kings.

1.—GIRLS' (5 years) FLAT RACE. 30 yards.
2.—BOYS' (5 years) FLAT RACE. 30 yards.
4.—GIRLS' (6 years) EGG AND SPOON RACE. 30 yards.
4.—BOYS' (6 years) FLAT RACE. 60 yards.
5.—GIRLS' (7 years) SKIPPING RACE. 60 yards.
6.—BOYS' (7 years) FLAT RACE. 60 yards.
7.—GIRLS' (8 years) FLAT RACE. 60 yards.
8.—BOYS' (8 years) FLAT RACE. 60 yards.
9.—DECORATED PRAMS.
10.—DECORATED BICYCLES.

SECTION B.—Open to Senior Scholars attending the Elementary Schools in Charlton Kings.

1.—GIRLS' (under 11 years) FLAT RACE. 80 yards.
2.—BOYS' (under 12 years) FLAT RACE (Handicap). 80 yards.
3.—GIRLS' AND BOYS' (Open) SACK RACE.
4.—GIRLS' (over 11 years) FLAT RACE. 100 yards.
5.—BOYS' (open) FLAT RACE (Handicap). 100 yards.
6.—GIRLS' POTATO RACE.
7.—BOYS' (under 10 years) FLAT RACE (Handicap). 80 yards.
8.—GIRLS AND BOYS' SLOW BICYCLE RACE.
9.—BOYS' (open) FLAT RACE (Handicap). 440 yards.
10.—GIRLS' (under 9 years) FLAT RACE. 60 yards.
11.—BOYS' (under 9 years) FLAT RACE (Handicap). 60 yards.
12.—GIRLS' BUN RACE.
13.—BOYS' APPLE-IN-WATER RACE.
14.—GIRLS' CLOAKROOM RACE.
15.—BOYS'. Final for " Jubilee Cup " kindly presented by Mrs. A. D. Mitchell.
16.—GIRLS'. Final for " Jubilee Cup " kindly presented by Mrs. A. D. Mitchell.

The Silver Jubilee of King George V in May 1935 was celebrated in Charlton Kings as elsewhere in the kingdom. Part of the programme of the day's events is shown here. The Revd R.H.M. Booth, the speaker at the opening ceremony, lived at Battledown Court, Oakley Road. He had been Rector of Elkstone, but from 1909 he had devoted himself to business and politics. He was, among his many other activities in public life, a county councillor for Charlton Kings and Chairman of the bench of magistrates, and, in the business sphere, a director and secretary of the Cheltenham Newspaper Company. The attractions listed here include bowling for a pig: the animal in question had been given by Shakespeare Shenton, owner of a cinema in Cheltenham, who lived on the London Road at the house that used to be the Beehive Inn (now bed and breakfast and holiday accommodation), just out of Charlton Kings, beyond Detmore Road. A Jubilee cup was awarded for the boy and girl winning the most points. They were presented by Mrs A.D. Mitchell, the wife of Arthur Mitchell of Glenfall House, who was connected with Mitchell and Butler, the brewery firm (not to be confused with the Mitchells of Ryeworth and Glenfall Farms and Ham Court). Later there were races for adults and a tug-of-war between teams from each side of 'The Brook', i.e. Ryeworth and the village. There was much more of a division and rivalry between the two populations than nowadays, so this contest would no doubt have been taken seriously. Cigarettes were given as prizes in men's competitions, something unthinkable today.

Opposite: The start of the annual Whit Monday walking race from the Ryeworth Inn to the Duke of York in the London Road, early 1950s. The race was popular until later in the 1950s. It was a family event, with a fancy dress competition for children included. The gentleman in the top hat about to blow his hunting horn to start the race is Albert Dowler Mitchell (see page 122), by this time living at Fontenelle, Sandhurst Road. After he gave up starting the race he presented the hunting horn and a series of photographs of past races to be put on display in the Ryeworth Inn. They are not there now, however, as a landlord in the 1970s unfortunately took them with him when he left. It would be pleasing to think that they may be returned one day as a reminder of this local event. (Photograph courtesy of the *Gloucestershire Echo*)

A fancy dress party for children and young people of Croft Avenue, Croft Parade and Croft Gardens, one of the many events arranged in Charlton Kings to celebrate the ending of the Second World War in 1945. The photograph was taken at the south end of Croft Gardens, before the way was cut through to Garden Road. The children's mothers have obviously used their ingenuity to produce costumes, probably not easy after several years of clothes rationing and shortage of materials, as the notice decorating the small child in the grass skirt reminds us. Back row, left to right: Leslie Davis, Michael Drinkwater, Jean Gibbons, Thomas Gaskins, Anne Taylor, Cyril Green, Ian Powell (an evacuee from London), Sheila Hawkins. Third row: Ivor Morton, Brian Hughes, Jean Thornton, Phyllis Drinkwater, ? Smith. Second row: Sybil Parker, ? Hughes, Christine Hughes, Pauline Hughes, Brian Thornton, Ken Stanley, -?-. Front row: Robert Hughes, -?-, Colin Hughes.

These mothers and young children are attending a 'Welfare Party' in Holy Apostles' Church Hall, *c.* 1959. The Charlton Kings Infant Welfare Centre was set up in 1923 largely because of General R.G. Burton of Bafford Grange, who called the inaugural meeting and acted as the first Chairman of the committee. His idea was that all mothers should be able to get advice on their pre-school-age children's health and development. The first medical officer, available to see any child recommended by the nurse, was Dr Barrett Cardew. The clinic was held twice a month, first of all in the St Clair Ford Hall, then from 1924 in the Six Ways Council Offices (now the Martial Arts College). By December 1923 sixty-eight mothers and seventy-five infants were on the books. In 1939, the Six Ways building being needed for use as a Food Office during the Second World War, the clinic moved to St Mary's Hall, in 1946 to the Baptist Hall, then to Holy Apostles' Hall in 1955–6. The last meeting of the Welfare Centre was in November 1986. The older lady, wearing a hat, in the back row is Miss Emily Statham, a member of the committee. She had been a teacher at the Girls' School, and also served as a governor of the Infants' School and a Sunday School teacher for many years. She died in 1980 aged ninety-three. (Photograph courtesy of the *Gloucestershire Echo*)

Hambrook Stores, Ryeworth Road (next door but one to the Ryeworth Inn), decorated for the Silver Jubilee, 1977. This was the last remaining shop in the Ryeworth area, and has since closed. The house has now been turned into flats and the single-storey annexe is a garage. In 1955 there were still several shops in Ryeworth, including a bakery and a boot repairer, but shopping patterns have changed here, as in so many other places.

A close-up of the plaque on Box Cottage marking the residence there of C. Day Lewis. It was unveiled by Jill Balcon. She is well known as an actress, and edited *The Complete Poems of C. Day Lewis* (Sinclair Stevenson, 1992).

The unveiling of the plaque on Box Cottage, 1983. The picture shows, left to right, Richard Morgan, Headmaster of Cheltenham College, Councillor Roy Marchant, Mayor of Cheltenham, Miss Jill Balcon, widow of C. Day Lewis, and David Phillips, Chairman of Cheltenham Civic Society, which, together with Cheltenham College, arranged for the plaque to be placed.

A crowd round a stall at the first Charlton Kings Festival, 1991. The festival was the idea of Mrs Margaret Walker and a small committee of helpers, and has continued to be held the first weekend in September each year since, gradually becoming more established and popular. There are concerts, flowers in the churches, a carnival procession, sometimes exhibitions, a flower and produce competition and a fair on the Grange Field, with stalls and displays. In the centre of the picture is the present Vicar of St Mary's, the Revd Graham Bryant. On the extreme right is Mrs Hazel Parkes, a member of the well-known Neather family (see page 114).

A display of Scottish dancing on the Grange Field at the first Charlton Kings Festival, 1991. The background shows how near to open country is the centre of Charlton Kings.

CHAPTER NINE
PEOPLE

A picture taken by J.A. Williams, a Charlton Kings photographer, whose address is given as Millbrook Place, on London Road between School Road and Hearne Road. The man's identity is not known. Tom Gosney, landlord of the Royal at the beginning of the twentieth century, kept a monkey, as did the landlord of the Ryeworth Inn, so it could possibly be one of them. It may, however, be the organ grinder who is remembered as a visitor to the village on Friday afternoons early in the twentieth century. He was described as an 'old, unshaven Italian' who spoke little English. He was accompanied by his wife, and had a box-organ and a monkey on the end of a 15-ft string. The monkey was, of course, very popular with children.

Above: Brevel Hey (or Brevels Haye), a sixteenth-century house in Brevel Terrace, photographed probably in the late 1890s, but certainly before 1914. Standing in the centre is Mrs Ann Buckle, whose late husband, Benjamin Buckle, was a member of the family which had owned the house since 1769, and after which Buckles Row and Buckles Close were named. She was born in 1820 and died in 1914 at the age of ninety-four. She is with her daughter, Elizabeth Annie White, who was married to Richard White of the Merry Fellow. After she was widowed in 1923 she lived with her mother-in-law. On the left is Elizabeth White's son, Frederick. The Buckle family owned Brevel Hey until 1925, by which time Elizabeth White and her daughter-in-law were living there. It was sold in that year to Mr and Mrs Leslie Bick, in whose family it remained until 1992.

Miss Cicely Hamlett, photographed in the early twentieth century. A member of an old Charlton Kings family, she lived at Conway Cottage in Church Street and ran a laundry, one of a good many in Charlton Kings, where she employed about a dozen women. A crèche was set up by two nurses in Copt Elm Road where, for a very small charge, babies could be left, enabling mothers to work in the laundries.

Charlotte (left) and Anne (known as Annie) James were the elder daughters of Benjamin James and his wife Elizabeth. In the 1851 census Benjamin was thirty-five years old, and his occupation was given as tailor and grocer. He and Elizabeth, thirty-four, lived at Brook Place, Cudnall (the houses in Cudnall Street just before the Brookway Road corner). His birthplace was given as Oxford, but Elizabeth was born in Charlton Kings. Their family in 1851 consisted of Edwin, aged thirteen, who was a tailor's assistant (having presumably left school at twelve years old), Evan Owen, aged twelve, Charlotte (ten) and Anne (eight months). Emily was born the next year, 1852. All three daughters were apprenticed to learn tailoring and dressmaking at Cavendish House in Cheltenham, walking there each day from their home. Charlotte and Annie later moved north to work in the tailoring section of a department store in Liverpool. Benjamin James died in 1861, aged only forty-five, Elizabeth in 1873 when she was fifty-seven, and their grave is in St Mary's churchyard.

Emily James was married at St Mary's Church on 1 June 1871 to John Morley Smith of Hewlett Road, Cheltenham. Her elder brother Edwin was one of the witnesses who signed the marriage register, and as Emily's father was no longer alive, it is likely that Edwin gave her in marriage at the ceremony. John was a painter and gilder, who, among other commissions, worked on the interior of Holy Apostles' Church, though his work there was lost in the fire of 1970. In All Saints' Church, Cheltenham, however, his decoration of the organ case and the clock on the west wall can still be admired. A family story has it that when the couple were courting, Emily was allowed to go to watch John at work as long as she took her knitting! The couple subsequently had four sons, three of whom served in the First World War (all returning safely), and four daughters.

An older Emily Smith, probably in the late 1920s. She was staying in Highbury, King's Heath, Birmingham, with a daughter who was married to the estate manager of Joseph Chamberlain, the great radical politician, MP, and several times Lord Mayor of Birmingham. A portrait of him, wearing his customary orchid buttonhole, hangs on the wall behind Emily. The dresses worn by the sisters in these photographs all look beautifully made, and it seems very likely that they demonstrate the family's dressmaking skills.

Members of the Hamlett family in the garden of Conway Cottage, Church Street, opposite the Merry Fello
c. 1919. The photograph was taken, as were many local ones at that time, by J.A. Bailey of Copt Elm Road. He w
in great demand for photographing family groups, weddings and sports teams, and his work was of high quali
Back row, left to right: James Bowen, Louie Taylor, Samuel William Greville Hamlett, Ernest Bowen, Ham
Bowen, Alfred Dyer, Ellen Taylor, Francis Brook Greville Hamlett, Francis W.J. Hamlett, Bert Portlock, Fan
Portlock, Fred Hamlett, Annie Hamlett. Middle row: Elizabeth Bowen, Elizabeth Hamlett, Winifred Hamle
Christina Hamlett, Cicely Hamlett, Winifred Hamlett, Amelia Hamlett, Ethel Hamlett, ? Bowen and daught
Christina Morris, ? Morris. Front row: Edward Bowen, Alfred Dyer, Molly Bowen, Robert Hamlett, Nancy Dyer, t·
brothers (details not known), Gwen Nunney, Jack Nunney, Hilda Nunney, Greville Nunney. All the above w·
members of the Hamlett family by birth or marriage ties. Samuel William Greville Hamlett was the undertaker
Church Street before Alfred Dyer (back row), his nephew, succeeded him (see page 61). Christina Morris (n
Dyer) had previously been married to G. Nunney (their children are in the front row), but he had died in·
drowning tragedy. Cicely Hamlett (known as 'Ciss'), the daughter of William Hamlett, was the sister of Elizabe·
Bowen and Samuel William Greville Hamlett (see page 110).

The Neather family, 1920. Neather is a well-known local name, and the family is connected by marriage to other local families. This group shows Frederick Neather and his wife Elizabeth with their children. Frederick Neather worked for the UDC in Charlton Kings, one of his duties being to look after their horses. Back row, left to right: Jack (oldest son), Mary (oldest daughter), Emma, Edith, Lill, Harry. Front row: Frank, Beatrice, Frederick, Elizabeth, George, Frances (known as 'Turk'). Frederick Neather and later his son Frank served in Charlton Kings Fire Brigade (see page 59) during its existence from 1902 to 1925.

F.J. Fry, generally known as 'Boss' Fry, was Headmaster of Charlton Kings School from 1897 to 1925. He is pictured here with his wife Carrie, and three children, believed to be nephews and a niece. There is a tent in the background, so the photograph may have been taken on a visit to the Scout camp like the one on page 38. Mr Fry succeeded Henry Folley, Headmaster for forty years, whom he had served as a pupil teacher, and he continued Folley's exceptionally good work. Many were grateful for the way their horizons were widened by his encouragement. He was also Churchwarden of St Mary's for many years. He was remembered fifty years later by a former pupil as 'a really caring man. I can see him in my mind yet, with his waxed moustache, never a hair out of place'.

Robert Buckley Podmore died in August 1907 aged fourteen. His father, E. Boyce Podmore, a noted huntsman and Master of the Cotswold Hounds, lived at Charlton House. Robert, known as Bob, his younger son, was also an excellent horseman, with skill and maturity beyond his years, and was the youngest Master of Hounds ever known. He inspired widespread respect, and his sudden death (possibly the result of previous head injuries sustained while riding) occasioned great distress. His family received nearly 500 letters of condolence and 150 telegrams from leading sportsmen and others all over the country. His funeral at St Mary's Church was attended by large numbers of people. Many members of the fire brigade were there, as Mr Podmore took a great interest in the Cheltenham Brigade and had presented them with a 'first-aid hose cart' (called 'Bob Podmore'). E. Boyce Podmore had connections with Vickers, the shipbuilders of Barrow-in-Furness, and Bob had accompanied his father on gun trials of the ship *Katori*, which had been built for the Imperial Japanese Navy.

The Japanese officers who had met young Bob Podmore were so impressed with the boy that they wished to give a memorial to him. On 18 April 1908 a memorial window on the south side of the chancel of St Mary's Church was unveiled, together with a tablet, stating that it was erected by Engineer-Captain T. Fujii and brother officers of the Imperial Japanese Navy, in loving memory of their dear friend 'Bob', their companion on the gun trials of HIJMS *Katori*, April 1906. The memorial erected by the Podmore family was then unveiled. The picture shows the ceremony, outside the east end of the church. The memorial includes the words 'A True Gentleman – a man – yet still a boy', taken from a letter written to Mr Podmore after his son's death. Among those in the picture are clergy (the Revd Edgar Neale was the Vicar), family members, firemen and Japanese guests.

Jesse Peacey (right) stands proudly beside his giant sunflower, October 1901. The picture was taken in his garden at Woodland Villa, Ryeworth Lane. The man on the left is probably the gardener, who should perhaps have the credit for the achievement. Mr Peacey was born in Charlton Kings in 1839 (Peacey is a well-known local name). He and his wife, Emma, had six children, among them Frederick John, who married Kate, daughter of George Mitchell of Ryeworth Farm (see page 121), and Alice Miriam, who married Richard Boroughs, son of William Boroughs, publican of Charlton Kings (see page 101). Jesse Peacey died in 1902.

Thomas Hopkins and his wife Beatrice in their garden at Elm Cottage, Brevel Terrace, 1930s. They were the parents of Miss Annie Hopkins (see page 44). Thomas Hopkins was originally from Leamington Hastings, Warwickshire, but came to Cheltenham as a young man, having left school at eleven years old, and took a job as a porter at Cheltenham General Hospital. There he met Beatrice Turner from Charlton Kings, who was a ward-maid there. She later went to work for Mrs Bagnall at Bafford House, and Thomas to work for Cypher's, the Cheltenham nurserymen. They married and lived near to Beatrice's parents' home, Elm Cottage, where they moved when her mother died. Thomas Hopkins later worked for private employers, including looking after a garden on the site of the present Rodney Road car park. This belonged to a surgeon living in Imperial Square, where there were no gardens behind the properties. He returned to Cypher's at the end of his career.

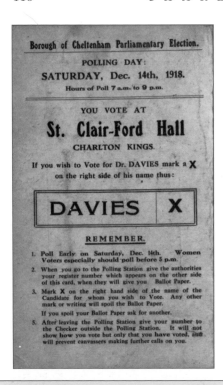

Borough of Cheltenham Parliamentary Election.

POLLING DAY:
SATURDAY, Dec. 14th, 1918.
Hours of Poll 7 a.m. to 9 p.m.

YOU VOTE AT
St. Clair-Ford Hall
CHARLTON KINGS.

If you wish to Vote for Dr. DAVIES mark a X
on the right side of his name thus:

| DAVIES | X |

REMEMBER.

1. Poll Early on Saturday, Dec. 14th. Women Voters especially should poll before 5 p.m.

2. When you go to the Polling Station give the authorities your register number which appears on the other side of this card, when they will give you Ballot Paper.

3. Mark X on the right hand side of the name of the Candidate for whom you wish to Vote. Any other mark or writing will spoil the Ballot Paper.

If you spoil your Ballot Paper ask for another.

5. After leaving the Polling Station give your number to the Checker outside the Polling Station. It will not show how you vote but only that you have voted, and will prevent canvassers making further calls on you.

A polling card for the Parliamentary Election of 1918 issued to Thomas Hopkins. The card was not the kind issued nowadays, which simply gives the voter's ballot number and details of the polling station, quite separate from party candidates' electioneering material. This card was issued by one of the candidates, Dr Richard Davies (see page 95), the Liberal Coalition candidate for the Cheltenham constituency. He is pictured with his wife on the inside of the card (below). Nowadays the custom is for elections to be held on a Thursday, but the polling day in 1918 was a Saturday. Voting was at the St Clair Ford Hall. The notes on the card state that 'Women voters especially should poll before 5 pm'. Perhaps this was because Saturday evenings became a little rowdy later on, and it was not recommended that women should be out and about. At this date all men over twenty-one were entitled to vote, but women were only eligible if over thirty. Dr Davies was unsuccessful in his attempt to become Cheltenham's MP. He was beaten by the Conservative, Sir James Agg Gardner.

Dr. R. Davies
LIBERAL COALITION CANDIDATE.

Mrs. R. Davies.

This wedding took place in September 1936 at Trinity Church, Cheltenham. The bride is Miss Christabel Doreen Prichard, the daughter of John Samuel Prichard, the 'Tailor of Gloucester', who had died two years previously. The bride's address is given as Pemberton, Albion Street, Cheltenham. This was the home of her grandfather, Philip Prichard, and he may be the gentleman to the right of the bride. The bridegroom is Alfred John Butcher of Lightpill, Stroud. On the far right in the back row is the bride's brother, Les.

Sections of the kerbstone round the grave in Charlton Kings cemetery of John Samuel Prichard, who was the original inspiration for Beatrix Potter's story *The Tailor of Gloucester*. He was indeed a tailor in Gloucester, though not, as the story has it, a poor old man, but a young and successful businessman when Beatrix Potter, who was staying with a cousin at Harescombe, near Gloucester, first heard the story. This told of an unfinished coat which was mysteriously completed overnight 'by the fairies'. In Beatrix Potter's version an embroidered waistcoat was finished by mice. The truth of the matter was less picturesque. It was the tailoring apprentices who, after a drunken Saturday night out, returned to the shop to sleep off their excesses. Being unwilling next morning to leave looking dishevelled as people were passing on their way to the cathedral service, they passed the time in completing the garment until the coast was clear. John Prichard later sold the business and became a teacher at Hardwicke Reformatory. He succumbed to tuberculosis, however, and later moved to Charlton Kings, living with his family at 1 Ashley Cottages, Croft Road (where Gilbert Ward Court now stands). There he had a summer-house in the garden, so that he could spend as much time as possible in the fresh air, the recommended treatment for tuberculosis at that time. He died on 24 February 1934 aged only fifty-seven.

Lewis Phillips on his four-year-old horse, The Parton, September 1928. They are facing the garden of Mr Phill
home, 4 Little Herberts (now 49 Little Herberts Road). There has been a cottage on the site since the sixtee
century, but the wide stone chimney is probably the only original part remaining. It has its back to the road
what we can see here is the end of the back garden. The cottage fronts on to a footpath, the road having been
aligned in the past. The cottage in the background was called Ealing Dene (now Southwold Cottage, see also p
19), which was originally two cottages, 1 and 2 Little Herberts. Mr Phillips' wife, Henrietta, took this picture w
a Kodak Brownie box camera. The name Little Herberts seems to derive from an old French word, 'herber
meaning harbourage or lodging, and has no known connection with a person called Herbert. Out of sight beh
the trees on the right is Herbert Villa, once the home of Horace Edwards (see page 58), which was la
demolished to make way for Chatcombe Close.

George Mitchell (1833–1905), seen here in the 1890s and looking every inch the prosperous farmer, was born in Hampshire. By 1856 he was described as a servant, living in Keynsham Place, Cheltenham, and he married Sarah Ann Wynn in that year. By the 1861 census the couple and their first child, Kate, were living at Ham Dairy Farm, and George Mitchell is described as a dairyman. A son, Walter, was born in 1865, and another daughter, Laura Ann, in 1868. By this time Mitchell was described as a farmer, and by 1871 he was at Ryeworth Farm (now called Little Manor, Greenway Lane), with four men working for him. Another son, Albert Dowler (see next page) was born in 1873, and two more daughters, Eva May and Frances Blanche, in 1874 and 1877 respectively. George Mitchell's wife died in 1878, aged only forty-three. He married a second time and had another son, Arthur George, who died aged seven in 1891. By 1900 all George Mitchell's surviving children were married and living in houses he had had built for them (some, such as Mottisfont and Tytherley, named after places in Hampshire, his childhood home). He was considering retiring from farming when, in 1905, he died after a very short illness. Coming from humble beginnings, George Mitchell had become, in the words of the *Cheltenham Examiner*, 'one of the oldest and most respected yeomen of this district . . . kind hearted and benevolent . . . [who] served his fellow parishioners in public affairs'. He had been an Urban District councillor, and actively campaigned for the Conservatives in parliamentary elections. As mentioned elsewhere, he also made one of his fields over to the Ryeworth Cricket Club.

Albert Dowler Mitchell, early 1950s. He was born in 1873, the fourth of six children of George Mitchell and his wife Sarah Ann of Ryeworth Farm. (His second name was the maiden name of his grandmother Ann.) When he was twenty-one, in 1894, and farming at Glenfall Farm, Albert Dowler married Minnie Florence Crump, a draper's assistant, of Cheltenham. The wedding took place at St Mary's Church and was reported in detail in the *Cheltenham Free Press*. In his younger years Albert Dowler Mitchell was a very good cricketer, and he can be seen in the Ryeworth team on page 74. In spite of encouragement from W.G. Grace to take the game up seriously, he followed his father's advice to stick to farming. In 1923 he left Glenfall Farm for Ham Court, where he farmed until 1947. He then retired and went to live at Fontenelle, Sandhurst Road. Like his father before him, and as his son was to do, Albert Dowler served on the Charlton Kings UDC, the three generations covering nearly 100 years service between them, and he was well respected for his contribution to the local community. He died in December 1962, aged eighty-nine, eight years after his wife.

George Wynn Mitchell was born in 1899, the only child of Albert Dowler Mitchell and his wife Minnie Florence. (His second name was the maiden name of his grandmother, Sarah Ann.) His mother was anxious for him not to follow in the family farming tradition, and he was sent to Dean Close School, proceeding to Woolwich for military training. He then served with distinction in the Royal Artillery in all parts of the world. In 1929 he married Enid Walker of Exeter, the first Mitchell family wedding not to take place at St Mary's, Charlton Kings, for over seventy years. The couple had three children, Diana, Timothy and Jillian. During the Second World War Lt Col George Wynn Mitchell was the officer-in-charge of coastal defences during the Siege of Malta. During this time his wife and two elder children were with him, and later they returned to England and stayed with Albert Dowler Mitchell at Ham Court. Meanwhile George Wynn was negotiating with the Free Norwegian troops at Scapa Flow, for which he was awarded the Norwegian Royal Blue Cross. On one occasion at this time he had the chance of a short leave, and travelled to Ham Court without giving notice of his arrival. This led to an amazing example of animal precognition. Apparently one of his black cocker spaniels insisted on being let out, and spent the day patiently sitting at the gate of Ham Court, refusing to budge. Then in the evening a taxi drew up and his master stepped out. . . . In 1960 George Wynn Mitchell and his wife retired to Charlton Kings and lived in a new bungalow in School Road. After the death of Albert Dowler the couple moved into Fontenelle, Sandhurst Road, which was then divided into two flats. George Wynn Mitchell died in 1973. His wife lived for another ten years, dying in North Wales in 1988.

Mary Isabel Holborow (née Butler) was born in 1855. She established the Gloucestershire Dairy and Creamery in 1876, before she married John Price Holborow. The firm's main centres were Whaddon Farm, and Bafford and Northfield Farms, both in Charlton Kings. Grazing was rented in Battledown, including land round The Camp. The firm stressed the importance of healthy cows and clean handling. Mrs Holborow remained the head of the firm until her death at the age of seventy-three in December 1928. By that time the business employed over 100 people and was a large landowner in Charlton Kings, owning Ashgrove and Bafford Farms; later Northfield and Ryeworth Farms were added. There are still Holborows on the Board of Associated Dairies, which took over the firm in 1993.

Rupert Hewitt Webb was the eldest son of H.A. Webb, co-founder of Webb Brothers. He served in the First World War, and in November 1919 joined the family firm and succeeded in building it up again after the difficulties of the war years. Like the others in his family he was a man of many interests and abilities. He was an excellent golfer and a keen pilot, a skilled photographer and an active Rotarian and Freemason. He was an officer in the Home Guard throughout its existence (see next page). A coal and coke business, sending truck-loads of fuel all over the country, was established, alongside the brick and tile side of the firm. In 1939, following the death of H.A. Webb, R.H. Webb became chairman of the company. In the Second World War, in contrast to the First, business flourished. Later a combination of political events and economic factors and the competition from mass-produced bricks caused difficulties, which resulted in the business being wound up.

The appeal in 1940 for volunteers to serve in the Charlton Kings Home Guard (originally called the Local Defence Volunteers) met with a very good response. This photograph shows members of one Charlton Kings platoon under the command of Lt R.H. Webb. At the beginning there were no uniforms except for arm-bands, and very few weapons, but gradually these were supplied. The Home Guard's duties included guarding the railway station and Dowdeswell Reservoir, and keeping a night-time watch from the tower of St Mary's Church; there were also training exercises and parades. Personnel changed as members left to serve in the forces or retired because of age. The Home Guard was 'stood down' and disbanded in 1944. Back row, left to right: -?-, Fred Mason, Joe Williams, the rest are unidentified. Second row: -?-, -?-, -?-, -?-, W. Tipper, Jack Staddon, Joe Manning, S. Winston. Front row: Alex Baylis, -?-, L.B. Schofield (who was a master at Cheltenham Grammar School), Lt R.H. Webb, -?-, -?-, R. Beekes, -?-.

The Charlton Kings and Leckhampton platoons of the Home Guard assembled before disbanding in 1944. Among the Charlton Kings men pictured are F. Bee, R. Beekes, F. Bloodworth, J. Brown, R. Bunting, T. Clarkson, A. Cooke, G. Enoch, T. Evans, H. Grace, L. Johnson, J. Loud, J. Manning, F. Mason, H. Peacey, K. Protherough, T. Protherough, G. Ryland, L.B. Schofield, T. Slee, R. Smith, R. Snell, J. Staddon, W. Tipper, R.H. Webb, B. Walters, J. Williams.

Mr Cyril Hollinshead, born in 1902, was a native of Lincolnshire, but he lived in Charlton Kings for some fifty years. He trained as a journalist and became assistant editor of the *Derby Evening Telegraph*. In 1938 he became editor of the *Gloucestershire Echo*, a post which he held until his retirement in 1967. He took a full part in civic life, and in 1945 he was one of a committee of five who were responsible for the founding of the Cheltenham Festival of Music, the first of its kind in Britain, pre-dating Edinburgh, Aldeburgh, Bath and the many others that have followed since. Mr Hollinshead remained on the Festival Board until his death. It was, however, as an amateur cricketer that Cyril Hollinshead was perhaps most widely known. From 1939 he played for the Gloucestershire Gypsies and continued to do so until three years before his death in November 1995, at the age of ninety-three. He was said to have become thereby the oldest cricketer in the world. This photograph was taken in 1990, when Mr Hollinshead was eighty-eight.

Mrs Marjorie Hollinshead, seen here outside Buckingham Palace, where she and her husband Cyril attended a garden party on 12 July 1967. She grew up in Derbyshire and after studying music became a professional singer. She met her future husband when he was a reporter on the *Derby Daily Express* and reviewed some of the concerts she took part in. After moving to Charlton Kings she continued singing, with the Cheltenham Bach Choir, and she was a founder member of the Charlton Kings branch of the Townswomen's Guild. She conducted its choir for many years. Marjorie Hollinshead died, aged eighty-nine, in January 1999.

Robert Stanley Gorrell Dent (1909–91) was born in Monmouthshire, but lived most of his adult life in Cheltenham, a great part of it in Charlton Kings. He joined the staff of Cheltenham Art School in 1935 after studying at the Royal College of Art, and, apart from war service with the Royal Engineers, remained there until his retirement. He became Principal in 1950, presiding over its expansion to become the Gloucestershire College of Art and Design and the move to Pittville from the centre of Cheltenham. When his duties allowed he travelled at home and abroad with his wife (a fellow-student from the Royal College of Art) and their two sons; this gave him subject-matter for many fine pictures. After his retirement in 1974 the Art College became integrated with the Cheltenham and Gloucestershire College of Higher Education. In 1991 an honorary MA was to have been conferred on him to mark his service to art education, but unfortunately he died before the degree congregation. A willow tree was planted in his memory at the Pittville Campus, and in 1997 HRH The Duke of Kent officially named one of the new Halls of Residence Dent House. Though professionally known as Stanley Dent or R. Stanley Dent, he was widely known as 'Reggie', dating from a mistaken guess by fellow-students as to what the 'R' stood for. He was greatly involved with saving the Pittville Pump Room from demolition after the Second World War, with the Cheltenham International Music Festival, and, in Charlton Kings, with setting up the Gloucestershire Wildlife Trust nature reserve on the former railway cutting between Cirencester Road and Little Herberts Road.

ACKNOWLEDGEMENTS

I am most grateful to the Committee of the Charlton Kings Local History Society for giving me the opportunity to compile this book, and also to all the contributors to the Society's publications, from which I have gleaned a lot of the information printed here; to my husband, Christopher, for writing the introduction and assisting in what has been very much a joint project; and to our editors at Sutton Publishing, Simon Fletcher and Sarah Moore, who have given us much invaluable advice and guidance. Above all I am grateful to all those listed below who have entrusted us with their photographs, given information or helped in any other way. This book could not have appeared without their co-operation. If anyone has been overlooked, I apologise; thank you all the same.

Miss Rosemary Ash, Mrs Marie Aston, Miss Diana Banks, Mr Don Bennett, Mr Jim Boulton, the Revd Graham Bryant, Mr J.J. Cooper, the Revd Ray Copping and the PCC of Holy Apostles' Church, Mr Barry Curl, Mrs Rosemary Daffurn, Mr Gareth Davies (Head Teacher of Holy Apostles' School), Mr and Mrs R.E. Davis, Mrs Doris Dent, Mr and Mrs Alan East, Mr David Edge, Fr Alan Finley (Sacred Hearts Church), Mrs Melanie Fletcher, Mr Alan Franklin, Mr Peter Grainger, Mr Raymond Green, Mrs Carolyn Greet, Mrs Judy Gresswell, Mr Ian Harris, Mr J. Hawkins, Mrs Ivy Hill, Ms Tina Hoban (The London Inn), Mr Roger Hollinshead, Miss Anne Hookey, Mrs Marjorie Hooper, Mr Ted Jones, Mr Colin Kingston, Mr Michael Mitchell, Mrs Yvonne Mitchell, Lt Col David O'Connor, Mrs Mary Paget, Mrs Hazel Parkes, Mrs June Pearce, Miss Pat Pearce, Mr Ron Phillips, Mrs Enid Phipps, Mrs Mavis Prout, Mrs D. Reeves, The Revd Roland Rempey, Mr John Ridley, Mrs Mary Southerton, Mr Ken Stanley, Mr Edgar Stickley, Ms Roz Taylor (Lilleybrook Golf Club), Mr Don Tipper, Mrs Maureen Vernon, Capt Ian Walkington, Mr Rupert D. Webb, Mrs Mary Wilcox, Mr Frank Withers, staff at the Gloucestershire Record Office and the Oxford Bus Museum Trust. I am grateful also to the Editor of the *Gloucestershire Echo* for allowing us to publish the photographs that are acknowledged in the text.

Every effort has been made to trace the copyright holders of photographs used in this book, and any omissions are unintentional. I apologise for any errors which there may be in the captions; it would be very helpful if readers could notify me, care of the Local History Society, of any corrections, or if they have further information, identifications or more photographs, which could perhaps be used in a future publication.

A charabanc full of ladies, probably St Mary's Mothers' Union or Mothers' Meeting members, about to set off on an outing, 1920s. The Revd Edgar Neale, in his boater, is next to the driver, and the party is setting off from the lychgate of St Mary's Church. The ladies may be en route for Tewkesbury, which was a favourite destination for such outings. Tea at a café would be a popular part of the proceedings.